"As soon as we read this manuscript, we knew we wanted Tom Bisset as a guest on our broadcast. Most everyone knows somebody who has left the faith. This first book we have seen on this subject is a real gift to the church."

David and Karen Mains
Chapel Of The Air

"For those who may be questioning their relationship with the Savior, this book will help sort it all out. For those of us who speak from the pulpit, it will help us once for all bury our packaged answers and begin to deal with real issues! Tom bisset has dared to ask why and I find his answers both biblical and believable."

Dr. David Jeremiah
Turning Point

"Tom Bisset has broken new ground in his book WHY CHRISTIAN KIDS LEAVE THE FAITH. It is a most relevantly refreshing analysis of the problem of prodigals and how to help them. It is must reading for every parent and for every other person who is concerned about the spiritual well-being of our children."

Dr. Tony Evans
The Urban Alternative

"Christians who leave the faith baffle the rest of us. How could they do that? Whose fault is it? But far more than questions are involved. There is also pain, pain for those leaving and for those left. Tom Bisset explores the questions and the pain and offers understanding and hope. By taking these people seriously and searching the Scriptures carefully, he has provided us a wonderful rendition of something that is best designated, I think, as holy wisdom."

Eugene Peterson
Professor, Regent College

To Mary Ruth, Tina

and Jon

Why Christian Kids *Leave* the Faith

TOM BISSET

THOMAS NELSON PUBLISHERS
NASHVILLE

First Printing, October 1992

Published in Nashville, Tennessee, by Thomas Nelson, Inc., and distributed in Canada by Lawson Falle, Ltd., Cambridge, Ontario.

Scripture quotations designated KJV are from the *King James Version*.

Scripture quotations designated NASB are from *The New American Standard Bible*, © The Lockman Foundation 1960, 1962, 1963, 1968, 1971, 1972, 1975, 1977.

Scripture quotations designated NIV are from *The Holy Bible: New International Version*, © 1973, 1978, 1984 by the International Bible Society. Published by Zondervan Bible Publishers, Grand Rapids, Michigan.

Scripture quotations designated NKJ are from *The Holy Bible: New King James Version*, © 1982 by Thomas Nelson, Inc., Nashville, Tennessee.

Scripture quotations designated TLB are from *The Living Bible*, © 1971 by Tyndale House Publishers, Wheaton, Illinois.

Cover design by David Marty Design

Library of Congress Cataloging-in-Publication Data

Bisset, Tom.
    Why Christian kids leave the faith / Tom Bisset
       p.   cm.
    Includes bibliographical references.
    ISBN: 0-8407-4547-8
    1. Ex-church members. 2. Youth—Religious life. I. Title.
BV4531.2.B574   1992
248.2—dc20   92–28677
                                        CIP

Printed in the United States of America
1 2 3 4 5 6 7 — 96 95 94 93 92

Contents

Acknowledgments

First books are never easy to write.

At first there is enthusiasm. This is soon followed by discouragement; certainty arises only to be trailed by doubt. One day you can't wait to get your thoughts in the computer. The next day you can't imagine how it will ever happen.

On this roller coaster one needs friends—people who will encourage, offer wisdom and also provide constructive criticism. I had such friends and I wish to thank all of them.

First, thanks to JOEL FREEMAN, local pastor and successful author, who suggested I write the book and then made the initial publishing contacts for me. I had ongoing help from the staff at WRBS who willingly read chapters as I went along and offered their insights; DAVID PAUL, newsman extraordinaire, was especially incisive in his comments. REV. DAVE SHIVE encouraged me from the beginning. He and his wife KATHY read the entire manuscript and made critically important observations. KEVIN COWHERD, a syndicated feature columnist for the *Baltimore Evening Sun* and my regular racquetball partner, was a constant source of encouragement. DR. DORIS MORGAN, director of the Metro-Maryland Counseling Center, read some of the manuscript and provided a number of helpful insights. My editor DAN BENSON was incredibly supportive and understanding. Most of all he was patient. Thanks as well to all the people who allowed me to interview them.

Finally, thanks to my dear wife MARY RUTH, without whose support and encouragement I would never have attempted such a project.

7

Introduction

People have wandered away from God from the beginning of human history.

Adam and Eve wandered. So did Cain. Demas forsook his faith for the city lights of Thessalonica. The American Puritans agonized over their wayward children and devised various schemes to prevent spiritual defection among their offspring.[1] Last week a friend called me, brokenhearted by his wife's rejection of him, their marriage and her faith in God.

Why does it happen? What causes a person who grew up in a Christian home to reject his or her faith? Few choices in life are more difficult or painful for all concerned. Yet people have made that fateful decision for centuries and continue to make it. Why?

Faith departures are not accidental or random events. People who walk away from faith in God do so for specific reasons. If we can learn what these reasons are, we can help those who struggle. We also can reduce the risk of faith rejection in others, including our children who may be potential faith dropouts.

In this book, I outline four fundamental reasons

why people leave the Christian faith. I discovered these reasons in basically two ways: 1. by talking with faith dropouts; and 2. by research in the literature of faith "exiting," as it is called by sociologists who study the "leaving phenomenon" in a broader context.

The evidence is there. We know why it happens. All we must do is see and understand, then act on what we know. To this knowledge and action we must add our own faith that God will help us as we offer love and guidance to these troubled souls. Surely the most comforting of all thoughts when thinking about faith rejection is that God cares more about wandering sheep than we do.

I have chosen an anecdotal/analytical style for this project. Using a combination of teaching and storytelling, I will try to explain why people leave the Christian faith. Where explanation fails, I hope illustrations will succeed. I then offer some practical suggestions about how parents and others can significantly reduce and even prevent faith rejection in their children. In each case, I follow the stories of leaving with these more analytical and practical chapters.

In the latter part of the book, I offer chapters on related topics, including a look at the tough issues and the pain that is part of this experience for everyone involved. I also look at the hope that belongs to every believing parent and I conclude with some comments about the ultimate solution to faith rejection.

But before I begin, I'd like to point out a few things.

1. *This book is not strictly about teenagers.* Certainly they are included, but they are not the focus. It is a book about people who grew up in Christian homes and chose to walk away from their faith at some point, no matter what their age.

Faith rejection is a process, not a snap decision.

Sometimes the flashpoint occurs in the teen years. For others, decades pass before they decide to walk away. One missionary's son I interviewed went through a spiritual convulsion in his middle thirties. "I never even knew I was mad at God until I was thirty years old," he said, shaking his head sadly. "I was so busy trying to serve God and do the right thing, I never stopped to think about my real feelings about my faith."

2. *This is not a book about people who grew up Nazarenes and chose to become Presbyterians,* or about Pentecostals who become Baptists or non-Charismatics who become Charismatic. These may seem like major shifts to parents, but they are really the outcome of a child's changing viewpoint. This is simply a part of the process of personal and spiritual change and growth.

A major shift in an essential doctrine is a different matter, of course. But so long as our children are involved in evangelical, Bible-believing fellowships, we should not view moving to another denomination as a loss of faith. Changing is not necessarily leaving.

3. *This is not a book about the doctrine of salvation.* I consider that a separate matter. If you want to read about whether or not a Christian can lose his or her salvation, you will need to put this book down and pick up another. I am concerned about "leaving the faith" experientially rather than theologically. What actually *happens* in someone's life that causes faith rejection? What is she feeling? What is he thinking? Why?

My personal view is that a true believer belongs to Christ forever. However, I realize that people who grow up in believing homes and have made professions of faith in Christ can wander far from God, and by so doing raise questions about whether they are truly in Christ. I leave that judgment to God who knows all things.

4. *Finally, this is a book of hope, not despair.* It's easy

to lose hope and turn inward in a search for what "went wrong." Examining ourselves is both scriptural and useful in this context. But it benefits no one when we become demoralized and begin to doubt that our children or other family members or friends will ever come back to the Lord.

More people have wandered away and returned than most Christians realize. Ask around your church. You'll be amazed at how many people you know who grew up in Christian homes yet once were far from God. For understandable reasons, it's the one story we prefer not to tell in public—so we wind up not telling it at all. And that is a loss to the body of Christ because the story of someone's return to the Lord is every bit as joyful and encouraging as the testimony of one's salvation.

So as you read this book remember: There is hope.

Why are you cast down, O my soul? And why are you disquieted within me? Hope in God, for I shall yet praise Him for the help of His countenance (Psalm 42:5).

Though the fig tree may not blossom, nor fruit be on the vines; though the labor of the olive may fail, and the fields yield no food; *though the flock may be cut off from the fold, and there be no herd in the stalls*—yet I will rejoice in the LORD, I will joy in the God of my salvation. The LORD God is my strength; He will make my feet like deer's feet, and He will make me walk on my high hills (Habakkuk 3:17-19, emphasis mine).

1

Why Do People Leave the Faith?

Jeff was sitting at the kitchen table drinking a cup of coffee when he got the bad news.

It was an evening just like any other. Nothing seemed unusual. He always brewed a cup of coffee when he got home from work. And he always sat in this same chair, sometimes reading the paper, sometimes thinking about the events of the day. But this cup of coffee would mark a watershed in his life.

Jeff's wife Lynn, an attractive dark-haired woman who looked younger than her age, came into the kitchen and began to move around, getting things ready for dinner. Then instead of setting the table, she pulled out a chair and sat down opposite her husband.

"Jeff, I have something I want to talk about," Lynn said simply.

Jeff put down the paper. He understood the meaning of that sentence. It was Lynn's warning flag. When she said it, something important was coming. A surge of nervous energy raced through his body. He looked inquiringly at his wife.

"Well, what have I done this time?" he asked with a trace of a smile.

"I don't believe in God anymore, Jeff. I think I've lost my faith." Lynn began to cry.

Jeff stared at her. He was too stunned to respond immediately. Didn't believe in God anymore? Lost her faith? The words sounded unreal and far away.

True, Lynn had seemed unusually critical of the church and some Christian friends lately, but Jeff considered that little more than a sort of crankiness that would pass. How was it possible that his wife could come to this point in her life without his being aware of it? How could she *not* believe in God?

When Lynn stopped crying, she began to tell Jeff the story of her journey away from the Christian faith.

"I've been angry about church for a long time," she said quietly. "I've tried to tell you, but you wouldn't listen. I've been struggling with my faith for a long time . . . doubting what I've been taught, wondering what I really believe."

Freed from the need to hide any longer, Lynn let it all out. "I know this is hard to believe, but I don't feel anything in church. It means very little to me. I attend and go through the motions, but I'm not there. I've been doing it mostly for you and the kids for the last year."

She paused momentarily, looking at Jeff for a reaction. Then she continued.

"There's more, Jeff," she said with increasing intensity. "I don't pray anymore and I don't read the Bible for myself either. I can't even open it."

Lynn went on to explain that she saw herself as someone on a journey to find out "who she was." She would continue that search no matter where it took her, she said, even if it meant the loss of her marriage and family.

There would be no more pretense. No more games. She would talk to her parents, who were Christians, and tell them everything (which she did). Her pilgrimage would continue, this time out in the open for all to see because what others thought no longer mattered to her.

Jeff told me Lynn's story on a cold, raw January day in a small Italian restaurant in Baltimore's Little Italy. He had called me the day before, insisting that we meet as soon as possible.

I sensed that something was wrong but he said nothing more on the phone. When I saw him, I *knew* something was wrong. He looked terrible. Slightly disoriented, he toyed with his lunch as he told me about Lynn. What had happened to her, he wondered. Why? How? What should he do or say? What was the meaning of this for his family and marriage?

We were longtime friends and, as the older Christian, I was supposed to have answers for him. I'm sure I offered him some insights. I had some words of comfort and I listened. That was good. But I'm also sure I failed my friend in many ways that day.

The simple fact is that while I had some ideas about why people reject their faith, I did not know with certainty. I knew that professing Christians—people who have made a confession of faith in Jesus Christ—sometimes walk away from their faith. I had seen that happen enough to know that growing up in a Christian home or attending a Christian school did not guarantee an ongoing Christian commitment.

I was shaken by Jeff's story, especially his pain and sense of helplessness. My inability to help him troubled me deeply. Questions rattled through my mind.

Why does it happen? How can something as lovely and appealing as the gospel of Jesus Christ become so unattractive and even repulsive that a person willingly goes against family, friends and all that is familiar and safe in order to get away from it?

Yes, people drop out. But do they have to? Surely there are discernable, understandable reasons why people who grow up in Christian homes choose to leave that faith. And just as surely, there must be ways, strategies, methods—call them what you will—to avert these tragic faith departures.

As I left the restaurant that gray afternoon, I made a commitment to myself. In the coming months, I would do my best to get to the bottom of the "leaving" question.

Tackling the Faith-Rejection Issue

I began by reading and researching materials related to faith rejection. I found little on the subject by Christian authors. On the other hand, I was surprised by the number of secular books, journals and articles dealing with faith "exiting," as it is sometimes called by sociologists. Other terms are also used, some of which I like and will adopt in this book: dropping out, defecting, leave-taking, disaffiliation, disengagement.[1]

Some of this material was helpful, but most of it was too technical to be of any use. What proved useful was seeing the methods used by these researchers. In most cases, their resource material came from interviews with people. Perhaps I should talk with dropouts. Why not? Here was the story from those who lived it. That would get me as close to the problem as I could get. Combined with my research, the personal stories of dropouts would put me well on my way to understanding faith rejection.

The project formed in my mind. I would seek out

people from Christian backgrounds who had decided for one reason or another to walk away from the Christian faith in which they had grown up or to which they had been converted at an early age. (People who convert later in life seldom drop out, an interesting subject in itself.) I would ask them basically two questions:

1. Why did you leave?

2. Was there anything anyone could have done or said that might have made a difference in your decision?

For nearly eighteen months I interviewed people of all ages. Most were from evangelical and fundamentalist backgrounds, although several were from mainline Protestant denominations. I tried to maintain an even balance between men and women. I did most of my interviews with European-Americans, although I had several lengthy conversations with African-Americans. Three people I interviewed were from foreign countries.

My sessions were mostly informal. Some of my material came in the form of written responses to a questionnaire I prepared for the project. Sometimes I took handwritten notes, scribbling furiously as people poured out their souls. At other times I taped the interviews and wrote down comments as we went along.

Perhaps my biggest surprise was the diversity of the faith rejection experience. Somehow I expected these exiting stories to sound basically alike, a kind of Jeff and Lynn with minor variations. But it was not to be.

I was sure, for example, that I would find an unhappy, poorly functioning home and/or church in the background of everyone who chose to exit. Yet some people I interviewed had grown up in apparently loving homes and caring churches. In some instances, people from the same family chose opposite paths.

I also learned that faith exiting can be varied in terms of end results. Some people who rejected their faith at age fifteen returned to a profound experience of faith by age twenty-five. Yet others, who turned away at age thirty-five, were still struggling and spiritually disillusioned at age forty-five.

Some people were openly hostile and bitter. They seemed determined to leave Christianity behind at all costs. They had embraced a lifestyle of sexual promiscuity, drugs, alcohol or other destructive personal behavior, as if by so doing they could destroy any prospect of going back.

Still others rejected their faith coolly. At some point along the way they simply decided that they wanted "nothing more to do with Christianity," as one businessman put it. His seemingly happy life without any religious commitments unsettled me.

As varied as these experiences were, general patterns of leaving emerged from my interviews. By piecing these together I was able to come to some specific conclusions about why people willingly walk away from something as important as their religious faith.

I also learned something about preventing faith dropout. When people tell you why they rejected their faith, they are also telling you its opposite—why they might *not* have rejected their faith had things been different. I will share those discoveries with you as well.

Maintaining a Healthy Perspective

At this point someone may object to this approach to the Christian faith because it appears to contradict simple faith in Christ and to usurp the place of the Holy

Spirit in teaching and securing believers in their faith. I don't think so.

Certainly it is possible to become too analytical, too sociological in the spiritual arena. That won't happen in this book. Be assured that I bring to this task the fundamental assumption that God alone redeems and keeps His people. I know that faith rejection is about spiritual warfare. I also believe that every person is ultimately responsible for his or her own spiritual condition.

At the same time I believe God wants us to understand ourselves as well as His salvation. Christians are new creations in Christ Jesus, but we are also flawed human beings who are capable of making a mess of things, particularly the challenge of becoming mature believers and trying to pass our faith on to our children. If we understand ourselves, our children and our faith while we trust in God to do His saving, keeping work, we have the right balance.

When I began my research, I thought that my carefully focused study along with personal interviews would bring me to clear answers about faith rejection. But I soon learned that faith rejection is a complicated business. For every answer there seemed to be an additional question.

Still, as each day passed, I knew a little bit more about faith rejection. I do not have all the answers. But I have some answers, and I will share them with you. While I am confident that my analysis of why people leave the Christian faith is essentially correct, no doubt I have overlooked some issues and questions and missed some helpful insights. Where I have done so, I hope you will allow a little room for me.

Why People Leave the Faith

Let me tell you in brief why people leave. I will explore the details in the following chapters, and I will also offer suggestions about how we can help our children and friends avoid that lonely, desperate walk away from their faith.

Why do people leave the Christian faith?

1. People Leave Because They Have Troubling, Unanswered Questions About Their Faith

They doubt that the gospel can answer the really tough questions of life. Typically intellectual and academic in nature, these questions can include theological questions as well as personal doubts about the Christian life. And there seem to be no answers, at least for these seekers after truth.

Unwilling to "just believe," they opt for "intellectual honesty." To do this they believe they must leave their childhood faith behind in order to find real answers in the real world.

Paul's story in the next chapter, which was not an interview but a real-life experience for me, will give you insight into the struggles of someone who eventually was overcome by his doubts and questions.

2. People Leave Because Their Faith Isn't Working for Them

Try as they might, these people cannot find the peace, joy, meaning or happiness the Christian faith promised them.

Simply put, the Christian experience of these people never quite seems to match their Christian beliefs. Disillusioned with the church and their fellow Christians, and ultimately disappointed with God, these believers go through a painful emotional and spiritual meltdown that leaves them unable to think or function as a Christian. They leave by default; they simply can't do it anymore.

In Chapter 4, Susan's story will take you through the tragic journey of a lovely, dedicated Christian young woman whose growing unhappiness with her role as a pastor's wife led to disastrous consequences leaving her embittered and disillusioned. I also call on Demas, Paul's disciple who "departed" for Thessalonica, for some surmised testimony about the power of spiritual disillusionment.

3. People Leave Because Other Things in Life Become More Important Than Their Faith

These dropouts slowly drift away preoccupied by business, pleasure, material ambitions, personal problems or other hard realities that are part of life itself. Their faith, which was once primary, becomes secondary. A secular view of life displaces their formerly sacred view of life.

You'll have a better idea of just how this slip-sliding away happens when you read Bill's story. A successful Christian businessman, Bill never intended to leave his Christian beliefs and lifestyle. Yet he drifted from his moorings until one day he looked up and his faith was a speck on the distant horizon. A frightening experience in the quiet hours of the early morning awakened Bill to his pitiful spiritual condition and began the journey that brought him back to the Shepherd's fold.

4. People Leave Because They Never Personally Owned Their Own Faith

These people have made few, if any, authentic faith choices in their lives. Instead, they conformed to the spiritual expectations of others, especially parents and church leaders. But they never consciously and willfully embraced Christ and the way of the cross for themselves. They were expected, even required, to believe—and they did.

Little wonder that when these well-meaning but robot-like practitioners of Christianity were faced with a life-shattering experience or other crisis of faith, they did not know what they believed, or if they believed at all. Paper thin on the outside and hollow on the inside, their faith collapsed like a house of cards in the storms of life.

Chris could tell you about that. Only he can't because he is long gone from the faith of his home and church. As it happens, I know Chris's story, at least up to a point. I'll tell it to you as a way of helping you understand how people can choose to leave the faith because they never owned it for themselves in the first place.

I'll also tell you about Margie, the MK (missionary's kid) who, until she was a young adult, never realized that other people had made all the important decisions in her life. When she finally took things into her own hands, her freedom became her bondage. Today she is a wanderer, gone from the love of her husband and her caring, brokenhearted missionary parents. Margie's faith never really belonged to her.

These are the four basic reasons people leave. If you will look and listen with care, you will find one or several of them somewhere in the story of everyone who leaves the Christian faith, no matter what their external circumstances.

Other factors affect the faith rejection process as well, although not as significantly as these four fundamental reasons. I examine a number of these in the final chapters of the book, including a look at the "X" factors in faith rejection and the role of personality in spirituality. I'll also let three brothers tell you their story—two stayed, one left. And you'll visit with two parents whose son dropped out and came back.

If we know, we can help. The challenge for Christian parents is to understand the reasons why faith rejection happens and then seek to prevent it from happening in their children's lives. The challenge for all believers is to know these things and reach out in love to those who are struggling, whether they are our children, family members or friends.

Our peace in all of this is knowing that the outcome of our efforts is in the hands of the Good Shepherd who cares more about wandering sheep than we ever possibly can.

2

Paul

Have you ever met someone who made an indelible first impression on you?

I remember the first time I saw Paul. He was moving through the lobby of an administration building during my first week in Bible school. He had the kind of looks and presence you noticed in a crowded room using nothing more than your peripheral vision.

In politics they would say that Paul was working the crowd, pressing the flesh. Only in Paul's case, he wasn't running for anything. He was being himself—smiling, friendly, introducing himself to shy underclassmen (and women) and generally making everyone comfortable.

My first thought was that he did not belong in a Bible school setting. He looked like Princeton or Yale. Classic good looks would be the right description: curly blond hair, blue eyes and two rows of Chiclet-like teeth that seemed to jump out of his mouth when he smiled.

As if being handsome were not enough, Paul was also tall, muscular and athletic looking. His movements were graceful and energetic. I remember too, that he was wearing a tweed sportscoat with blue jeans. You simply couldn't miss him.

No way this guy can be spiritual, I thought to myself. *No way.* With the remarkable x-ray vision of a first-year Bible school student, I looked right through his dazzling exterior and saw a heart puffed up with pride and self-centeredness.

I did not meet Paul that evening. In fact, I avoided him. Even though I was a lowly freshman and he was a junior, I knew that I did not need the friendship of vain, worldly upperclassmen. Such people could only pull me down from the spiritual heights I had already attained and would divert me from the heavenly city upon which I had already fixed my gaze. Bible school was a place for serious people . . . like me.

My next encounter with Paul was in the school dining room. I was finishing dinner when he walked up to our table and began talking to a student sitting opposite me. He leaned over and said something about "getting going." As he bent forward, I saw a shiny object in the upper outside pocket of his coat: the gold-edged pages of a New Testament! I learned later that he and this student were involved with other students doing street evangelism. My first impressions of Paul were beginning to undergo revision.

Two weeks later I met Paul one-on-one for the first time in the student union. I was playing ping-pong and he came in with several friends. He must have been watching me (with his peripheral vision, no doubt), because he challenged me to a match after I had dispensed with my opponent.

He was good, but not good enough. In those days ping-pong was my game. (Today, it's racquetball.) I had a high school championship under my belt, and this was my chance to make an indelible freshman impression on a Big-Man-On-Campus—while his friends watched, no less. We played two games (that was against the rules while others were waiting to play, but when a freshman beats a BMOC junior in front of his peers, you can do those things), and I did not resist—after all, the more games won, the more fame gained.

Paul took the losses with a grace which impressed me. I was not a good loser and I admired people who could shake hands, smile and congratulate someone who had just beaten them in a sport. After the second game we talked briefly, made an informal agreement to play some more ping-pong at a later date and went our separate ways.

In the two years that followed, Paul and I became good friends. We did not become close buddies—the age and class differences probably dictated that. But we got to know each other pretty well. We talked theology, sports and just about any other subject that interested us, including girls. He was a classy, bright guy who loved the Lord and planned to serve God in the pastoral ministry.

A Fervent, Committed Believer

Allow me to tell you a little more about Paul. I include this incident because I think it will give you a feel for his Christian commitment. When you hear the rest of Paul's story, I believe this anecdote will help you understand that even the strongest, most dedicated Christian can begin to have doubts about his or her faith, start a questioning process and ultimately choose another path in life.

Not far from the Bible school, on a secondary street, was a slightly seedy supper club which featured a speaker's platform in the dining area. During the socially turbulent '60s (when I attended Bible school), this supper club invited speakers of every stripe and persuasion to present their views, after which the house guests could question the speaker.

Through a series of events, Paul managed to get himself on the speaker's list. If they could tout Communism in this club, why not Christianity? He invited several of his friends to join him in this venture, including me. We spent weeks thinking and talking about how we would handle this opportunity. We prayed a lot too. Those prayer meetings are among my fondest memories of my Bible school years.

Our big night at the club came and went. I suppose it was like any other evening for the customers. Just one more fool babbling about something. We presented the gospel simply and then answered questions. (I was asked about the origin of sin ... go figure.) One of the guests was a Jew who stood up and roared against us and Jesus. I was thrown off balance momentarily by the force of his personality and the shock of hearing someone whose religious views were the opposite my own speak with such conviction.

What I remember especially about Paul that evening was the attractive, winsome way he spoke of his faith. You could almost want what he had by looking at him. He answered questions with a graceful simplicity that amazed me. To one man, who called him a narrow-minded fundamentalist, he replied, "If I am a fundamentalist, then the apostle Paul was a fundamentalist. Read what he wrote and you'll see I'm only repeating what he said. If you want to argue with my view of God and the Scriptures, you'll have to argue with the apostle Paul first." I had never heard anyone turn a criticism of Christianity around so simply.

We left the supper club that night walking on air. We were certain we had declared God's truth in a way that would make everyone who was there aware of his or her sin and God's simple plan of salvation. Several of the guests spoke to us afterward of their appreciation for our style and message. We walked back to school and committed the evening to God in prayer.

For me, that was Paul at his finest. I don't know how the joy of Christian fellowship and service could be any better than what the four of us experienced in the events associated with that evening. We were young and full of faith and hope. We rejoiced in the thought that God had used us to declare his good news to lost men and women.

Can you understand the sadness I feel when I tell you that today Paul wants nothing to do with Christianity? No, he did not go into the pastoral ministry. Instead, he chose the business world and became a stockbroker with a big firm, a beautiful home and all the trappings. As pleasant and gracious as ever, Paul has long since dismissed the faith of his home, church and Bible school.

Incredible! How could such a person find his way to a place in life where he no longer knows or cares what he believes about Jesus Christ? Even in my strongest moments, I am shaken by the thought of Paul, friend and fellow student of the Scriptures, smiling, successful and unconcerned about God. It just doesn't seem possible.

When the Foundation Begins to Tremble

I haven't talked with Paul for years. But I know something about what happened. He told me some of it himself and I heard the rest from others. It is the story of a young man whose beliefs were undermined by a series of events, none of which was catastrophic, but all of which, when combined, brought him to a deliberate decision to walk away from the Christian faith.

When Paul graduated from Bible school, he decided that he would get his bachelor's degree from a state university and then go to seminary to prepare for pastoral ministry. He could transfer enough credits from Bible school to enter as a junior. In two years, he would have both a Bible school certificate and a B.A. from an accredited university.

"I want to face the real world," he said when asked by friends why he wanted to go to a secular university. "I need to know how unbelievers think. I want to understand what makes them tick."

Paul decided to major in psychology. He was unafraid of the world's wisdom, he said, because he knew what he believed. To grapple with the "mind doctors," as he called them, was to better understand people and society. He believed, as well, that a degree in psychology from a major state university would give him added credibility among unbelievers, as well as an advantage when preaching the gospel.

As well-schooled as Paul was in the Scriptures and in his Christian beliefs, he was unprepared for the unbelief on the university campus. His professors were tolerant of him but unyielding in their view that a man of "faith and myth" could never be a true intellectual. His fellow students considered him decent but quaint. In a time of social change and upheaval, he was out of touch with the real world.

Determined to be morally strong as well as intellectually honest, Paul plunged ahead with his studies even though he was becoming increasingly unsure of himself. He sought help from various Christian writers and thinkers, as well as campus student ministries.

One night after wrestling with inner conflicts about Christianity and psychology, he called a leading Christian apologist (whom he did not know personally) and talked long distance with him for an hour and a half. Cheers for a nationally known theologian who had that kind of time for an unknown college student struggling with his faith!

Paul finished his degree with a major in psychology and remained committed to his Christian faith even though, as he put it, "the ground of his beliefs had trembled under him." He had survived the intellectual doubts secular higher education had forced upon him. But just ahead were more practical tests of his faith which would revive his intellectual doubts and raise questions which would change his view of the Christian faith.

Unanswered Questions, Unsettling Doubts

During spring break in his senior year, special evangelistic services were held at Paul's home church. Paul's pastor invited him to take charge of counseling those who wanted to make a decision for salvation during the meetings. He would be responsible to both train counselors and talk with people who were seeking salvation or spiritual counsel. He would also do some follow-up ministry with those who made a profession of faith. Paul accepted.

Paul took his responsibilities seriously and did his work well. What he did not handle well was the refusal of the evangelist to counsel with people who had come forward to receive Christ. As soon as the service ended, the evangelist left the church and went to his hotel or to a restaurant, leaving Paul and the others to talk with those who had come forward after each meeting.

Disturbed, Paul confronted the evangelist who told him that he was "called to preach, not teach." Counseling those who came forward in response to his message was the responsibility of others with different gifts. Besides, if he took time to talk with people after each meeting, he would be exhausted before the special services were completed.

Normally easygoing, Paul reacted strongly. Were these revival meetings a job for a professional Christian gunslinger or someone with an evangelist's heart for people? How could a man of God be so disconnected from the message he was preaching?

Years later, Paul would look back to this experience and realize that unknowingly he had already begun to question his fundamentalist heritage as well as his intellectual beliefs. Soon he would be questioning the Christian faith itself.

Back at the university shortly after spring break, Paul made a decision: He would stay at the university and earn a master's degree in psychology. He could do it in a year if he went to summer school. Then he would go to seminary. Something in him wanted more of the hard realism of the secular campus and the mind-stretching atmosphere of the university classroom.

His parents, who were Christians, were uncomfortable with this decision but made no attempt to dissuade him. His pastor, however, took a different view. One Sunday after church in early summer, Pastor Jones asked Paul if he could stop in his office following the service that evening. He had some things he wanted to talk about.

"I'm concerned about you, Paul," his pastor said quietly but strongly. "I understand you've decided to earn a master's degree at the university instead of going on to seminary. I hope you don't mind me saying this, but as your pastor, I feel I must tell you that I don't agree with that decision."

Pastor Jones paused, looked down at his desk, then up again. "Paul, I think you're getting caught up in psychology. You're not the same young man who went off to Bible school five years ago. If you continue to go down this psychology road, you're going to get yourself into serious trouble spiritually."

Paul had never argued with his pastor and did not do so at that point, though he felt like it. Instead, he said simply that he appreciated his pastor's concern and would think things over, but his mind was pretty much made up about the master's in psychology.

What happened next marked one of several turning points in Paul's faith journey.

"I'm sorry to hear that, Paul," his pastor said with increasing agitation. "I had hoped you would be more open to what I had to say." He stopped momentarily, looked at Paul and took a deep breath.

"I have something I need to tell you," he said. "This past year, the deacons talked about making your seminary expenses a home missions project of the church. We have already decided to underwrite all of your tuition. We thought it would be an excellent choice for our home missionary efforts."

Pastor Jones paused again as if what was to come would be painful for both of them. "But if you stay at the university, Paul," he said, "I will recommend that the board find another home missions project."

Paul was surprised by the news of the board's interest in his seminary expenses, but even more taken back by his pastor's comments about changing the decision. Angered, he replied sharply that he "did not wish to be bought" by the church and did not care what the church did with its home missions money. He stood up, excused himself and walked out of his pastor's office.

Paul took his master's in psychology at the university, then he attended seminary for one year after which he dropped out. He couldn't do it, he said, at least not at the moment. Maybe later. Coming from the university environment, seminary seemed emotionally flat and intellectually cramped. What's more, he just didn't seem to fit in. He was asking questions while other students were offering answers. How ironic. Once a Bible school graduate shaken by entering university, he was now a university graduate shaken by entering seminary.

Within five years, Paul was a disillusioned faith dropout. To get to that point, he traveled across a spectrum of religious belief from fundamentalist to liberal, looking for a church where he "fit," including a brief try at Catholicism. Once a natural, happy place for Paul, church had become the least comfortable place in his life.

In the end Paul opted for what he called "benign agnosticism." He didn't know what he believed. He wasn't hostile to the Christian faith (though I think he was angrier than he knew or let on). He just didn't want the old, familiar faith anymore. He doubted many of its tenets and he had little confidence in the people who claimed to practice them. Little wonder that he walked. How can you be intellectually and morally honest *and* be committed to a faith you no longer believe in?

Facing Tough Questions

Now come the tough questions. Did Paul have the faith baton firmly in his hand? Was the transfer good? Yes! He had it! I know because I was there when the fire burned within him. I felt the heat of his passion for God. If what he had wasn't spiritual reality, what is?

Somehow, as he got into the race and began to run those long, hard laps, the baton slipped from his fingers. One short decade after he stood on that small stage proclaiming Christ in the boisterous, pagan atmosphere of a supper club in north Chicago, Paul had given it all up.

More tough questions. How could such a thing occur in the life of this young man? Why was he unwilling or unable to see what was happening to him? Why did he not consider his torment and choose the way of Christ by simple faith in the same way he once had invited people on the street to turn away from their sin and choose Christ?

When I sift through Paul's story, I think I see several reasons why he walked away from his faith.

First, Paul got away from his commitment to a personal relationship with Jesus Christ. Somewhere, somehow, he allowed prayer, Scripture study and meditation to diminish and ultimately disappear from his Christian experience. I know this because he told me he could not so much as open the Bible or pray. For him, the heavens were "brass" and the Scriptures were "stone."

Wait. This is not one of those simple answers Christians sometimes use to explain the problems of life. This *is* one of the reasons Paul began to lose hold of his faith. Christians are called to a life of personal fellowship with God. Throughout the ages, Christians have believed that without this inner relationship with God, there is little hope of success in the Christian life. Those of us who grew up in Christian homes recognize this as one of the basic requirements of the Christian life. We learned it line upon line, precept upon precept, just as Paul did in his home and church.

We also know how hard it is to faithfully walk with God in this way. Things happen. Problems, difficulties, success, doubts, questions—these and a dozen other things conspire to break down our commitment to maintain this personal fellowship with Christ.

Paul also began a process of questioning certain beliefs and practices of the fundamentalist faith in which he had grown up. He was especially troubled by what he called the "dodging" game: putting heads in the sand when tough questions came, resorting to religious clichés when faced by problems, refusing to face facts. "Fundamental churches," he concluded, "are full of people using the Bible to hide from the truth about themselves and the realities of life."

Intellectual doubts also began to plague him. Unlike dropouts whose earliest doubts are related to philosophical issues (the existence of God, science), Paul's intellectual doubts came after he was already aware of his growing spiritual disillusion. My guess is that his strong Bible/theology background helped him deal with the intellectual challenges to his faith, at least for a while.

But even this well-constructed defense against unbelief began to crumble toward the end of his faith struggles. Once his doubts about practical matters in the Christian life began to win the day, his intellectual doubts began to increase.

In a domino-like sequence, Paul began to raise questions about other issues such as the narrowness of conservative theology (liberal theologians had truth too), the correctness of certain doctrinal views (was verbal plenary inspiration correct or even necessary?), the reactionary attitudes of conservative Christians toward the physical and behavioral sciences (you can't be honest and avoid such things as evolution and psychology).

It seems to me that these seeds of doubt were planted in Paul during his university experience. There he faced new, unsettling ideas about his faith, himself and life itself. He viewed all of these challenges as worthy of his consideration, not realizing that even as he wrestled with them these ideas were burrowing deep in his mind and heart. Later experiences, such as the ones with the evangelist and his pastor (as well as others), stirred these submerged doubts and questions and gave them a renewed force within him.

Was attending a secular university a mistake for

Paul? I do not know. Others like him have gone through secular universities and come out spiritually strong. How can one be sure that if Paul had gone to a Christian college and then directly to seminary that he would not have come to these same conclusions later in life? University may simply have speeded up the process for him.

What I am certain about is that Paul's questions and doubts eventually overcame him. Naming these few is unfair to him; he was intelligent, knowledgeable, honorable. He did not let go of his faith without an enormous, pain-filled struggle that involved his mind, his heart and his conscience. Still, he let go. During his struggles, Paul insisted that above all he must be a "real" person, that he must be intellectually and emotionally honest about truth as he understood it. Whatever it was, he would embrace it. In the end, he believed he could not be either emotionally real or intellectually honest and remain committed to the faith in which he had grown up. And so this marvelous young man, one of the best and brightest Christians I have known, walked away and gave himself to something other, something lesser than the Christ he once loved and served.

People leave the faith of home and church because they have troubling, unanswered questions and doubts about that faith. Some are intellectual in nature, others practical. In time, these questions and doubts grow into disbelief which in turn produces faith exiting. It is a story that has repeated itself in all places and all generations where the church of Jesus Christ has existed.

Few choose to depart as radically as Paul. His personality, intellectual makeup and circumstances combined to undermine his faith to an unusual extent. In spite of this, I will not take him off the hook. He made his own choices and he is responsible. But there are factors which, had they been different, surely would have made a difference in the way Paul handled his faith struggles. And surely that would have made a difference in the outcome.

People have questions. Christians doubt. They doubt their faith, its relevance to life, its truthfulness and reality, and its ability to produce what it promises. It happens more than you think. Younger Christians and older Christians, pastors, missionaries and Christian workers, business people and teachers, teenagers, parents, preachers' kids and missionaries' kids. Few believers get through life without real doubts at some point along the way.

The good news is that questions and doubts hurt no one. In fact, wrestling with our doubts and questions can make us strong, healthy Christians. Paul's story is not about the dangers of doubting. It's about the dangers of Christians—parents, pastors, teachers and friends—not understanding and not dealing with doubts and questions. Left unnoticed or unattended, questions and doubts can become dangerous and deadly to the life of faith.

3

A Faith of Evidences and Explanations

I like family histories. Tell me about my maternal grandfather who left Holland alone at the age of eighteen and when you are finished, I will ask you more questions. Why did he leave? What was he like? What happened? I want to know.

I have the same interest in the paternal side of my family. There you will find an ample supply of preachers and missionaries. Also a politician, a foreman in a Scottish steel mill and an English gent who lost everything he owned—houses, lands and money—in one private horse race with the owner of another horse. That event, retold ominously through the years, produced a fierce opposition to gambling in our extended family.

Fundamentalists and evangelicals have a family

history too. We have a past that is part of who we are today. I am interested in my spiritual heritage. That is one reason I completed a graduate degree in American religious history at Johns Hopkins University. I wanted to know. Who am I? Where did I come from? What happened back there?

While my interest in religious history was partly academic, it was also personal. I wanted to know in the larger, historical sense, why fundamentalists and evangelicals of an earlier era had such a hard time entertaining and answering questions. Why had Paul never wrestled with the difficult social and intellectual issues that finally undermined him? Why had he come to Bible school (like most of us) certain that he knew most of the answers to life's hardest questions?

It was not long before I began to understand why an earlier generation of Christians had such an aversion to a thinking, question-answering faith. I also began to see why Christian parents of that generation had so much difficulty dealing with the doubts and questions which became an everyday part of their children's lives.

Anyone for a little history?

The Roots of Fundamental/Evangelical Christianity

A hundred years or so ago, our spiritual forefathers (and mothers) started a religious revolution by rebelling against the growing theological liberalism in American churches. The Bible was being questioned and basic Christian doctrines were being dismissed. Church leaders seemed more concerned about social problems than sin problems. Evangelism and missions were being pushed into the background.

Faced with the challenge of turning back the forces of theological liberalism, resistance forces began to organize in churches small and big, urban and rural. Battles broke out in seminaries and denominations; breakaway professors founded new conservative seminaries. "Independent" churches sprang up. New denominations formed. A new movement of specialized ministries outside the church began to flourish. Publishing houses opened. Books and pamphlets appeared (the classic revolutionary tactic).

One widely distributed pamphlet called, "The Fundamentals," crystallized the issues—Christians should get back to basics, back to the fundamental doctrines of the Scriptures. God's Word must be honored and obeyed. Missions and evangelism must be central in church life. Wealthy Christian businessmen financed the publication and distribution of millions of these pamphlets throughout the United States in the first decades of the twentieth century.

The opposition, grinding their teeth, dismissed this Bible-centered, back-to-the-basics movement as one more "ism" come to plague the church—fundamentalism. One critic called it an intellectual virus from the countryside, not realizing that the first signs of the revolt could be found in huge lunchtime prayer meetings in the nation's largest cities.

Newspapers, which often carried the story of this holy war on their front pages, described the adversaries in starkly contrasting terms: On one side were denominational leaders and theological intellectuals offering a thoughtful, socially sensitive Christianity. On the other were rabble rousers and simpletons trying to take American Christianity back to the eighteenth century.

The characterizations stuck. In the public's mind, liberals were reasonable, thinking people who were trying to make Christianity relevant to the modern era while fundamentalists were simpleminded, backwoods folks who believed the Bible because the cover said, "Holy Bible."

A major outcome of this bitter struggle between liberal and conservative Christianity was the development of strong anti-intellectual feelings among fundamentalists and evangelicals. After all, was it not the seminary professors, the academics and the intellectuals who were responsible for promoting theological liberalism? If that is what a good education does for you, who needs a good education? Who needs philosophy and logic when the outcome is loss of faith in God and His Word? Questions? Why ask why? Repent! Believe! All else is folly.

And so for people who grew up in fundamentalist and evangelical homes, questioning became taboo. Not simple factual questions, of course. Large, philosophical questions. Is God really there? Can we really know or is it all just a leap in the dark? How do I know I can trust the Bible? How do I know my faith is not a psychological crutch, a mental game I'm playing? What about evolution, anthropology and geology? And what shall I do about other religions?

This no-questions-please approach dominated fundamentalism from the first decade of the twentieth century to the early 1950s. If you grew up in a fundamentalist home or attended a fundamentalist church or college at any time during this period, you knew without being told that questions and doubts were not welcome at home or church. You believed. The ungodly doubted.

This approach worked for a while. The fundamentalist revolution was an apparent success. Theological liberalism slowed while theological conservativism surged. Conservative denominations grew and independent churches flourished. But the battle was not over. For, unknown to these earnest Christians, another revolution was on the horizon, one that would challenge fundamentalism's most basic beliefs.

The Emergence of Doubt in American Society

Beginning in the decades of the '50s and '60s (though its roots reached back into the '40s and '30s), a new way of thinking began to emerge in American society. The basic premise of this new way of thinking was that all of life was open to question. Doubt your beliefs! Don't let them tell you what to do. Think! Question authority! Come to your own conclusions and live your own life! You couldn't assume anything: not in politics, education or business, not in morality, marriage or music. And especially not in religion. Certainty was out; uncertainty was in.

No idea could have been more diametrically opposed to fundamentalism.

For fundamentalists, the frightening part of this new challenge was that you could run but you could not hide. There was no way to prevent these ideas from getting into your home or your church because ideas go where people go. Everywhere you looked and listened, doubt was in the air. Public and private education, radio and television, literature, the business world, government, the entertainment industry—society itself.

Fundamentalists responded in basically two ways: 1. They became increasingly conscious of doctrinal correctness; and 2. they put their hands over their eyes. There were exceptions, of course, but in general, making sure no doctrinal errors crept into the church and pretending that no problems existed became the basic line of defense against the new unbelief.

In church, fundamentalist pastors and Sunday school teachers met with little doubt about their preaching and teaching (although more doubt was there than anyone realized). After all, people did not attend church to doubt or question. Or to talk to each other about such things. Church was the place you went to have your faith reinforced.

But at home, the new thinking became everyday business. Parents felt pressures they had never experienced before. Pressures from questions. Academic questions. Social, cultural and ethical questions. Racial questions. Sexual questions. Music and entertainment questions. Questions about the length of your hair and the cut of your clothes. Dozens of questions. And doubts.

Most parents responded in the best way they knew how. They answered the questions with an earnest simplicity rooted in their own authentic, joyful experience of the Christian life. They had believed by faith. Why couldn't their children? But to their children, such talk sounded strange, almost like a foreign language. No one in their world talked that way.

Some parents were less tolerant. They either ignored the questions and doubts or dismissed them. "I see no problem here" and "I don't want to talk about it" became their stock responses. After all, good Christians don't question. They trust. They believe God and His Word.

Caught between parental misunderstanding and pressure from their peers, Christian kids soon stopped asking questions. In some cases they stopped talking altogether at home and church. Instead, they talked to their teachers and friends, most of whom spoke the new language of doubt fluently. Tensions mounted.

Throughout the decade of the 1960s, spiritual confusion and interpersonal conflict were the norm rather than the exception in Christian homes and churches. Two different ways of thinking about life had met head-on in a spiritual and cultural collision of epic proportions. The outcome was the alienation of many children from their parents. This alienation was accompanied by enormous personal and family suffering, much of which can still be felt today.

Happily, that conflict is largely past. Yes, some Christians are still trying to live as if nothing has changed, pretending that there are no questions worthy of serious consideration so far as dedicated believers are concerned. Some children still grow up in intellectual and cultural environments more like the '50s than the '90s. And sadly, these children will pay the same price their predecessors paid. Some will make it through but many will grow up struggling with their faith. Some will become alienated from their families and churches. Others will become bitter, harsh enemies of the Christian faith. Parents will grieve and wonder why.

For the most part, however, evangelicals today understand that the world in which we live and move and have our being is changed forever from the wonderful, simpler days of the '30s and '40s. Now the Christian faith must be understood, believed and lived out in a society permeated by doubt. To not answer questions or reply thoughtfully to the doubts and questions of our children and friends in today's world is to do them and ourselves an unspeakable disservice.

Dealing With Those Faith-Testing Questions

So then, how is all of this to be accomplished? How do everyday Christian parents deal with the doubts and questions that intrude daily into the lives of their children? If we can't run or hide, must we all have doctorates so we can smugly answer the questions and resolve the doubts?

No, not at all.

In the first place, our attitudes are as important as our answers. If we are open toward our children—if we let them know that we understand why they are questioning and doubting—we begin to defuse the issue. They know it's safe to ask questions and they're reassured by our confidence. See, Dad's not afraid to talk about it! Mom knows!

Sometimes parents can raise questions before they come up. When our children were growing up, my wife and I occasionally would look for openings where larger faith issues could be inserted into conversations. Sometimes we'd pose questions and get our children to defend themselves against us playing the role of unbelievers. We wanted them to know that we knew, that we too had wrestled and struggled with these same issues. We wanted them to know that we welcomed their questions.

Our logic was basic. Why should we allow our kids to sit in some classroom wondering if their parents were aware of the real issues, of the really big problems and questions out there? That thought in itself would be faith undermining and could even become faith destroying. I'm confident that more than once amid the doubt in a high school classroom our kids said to themselves, "Oh yeah, I know about this. We talked about it around the dinner table."

We told our children about the essentials of our faith and that we believed them absolutely. But we also told our kids we weren't absolutely sure about everything. We said we had thought a lot about those things and knew what we believed, but we might be wrong. We admitted that some very smart people disagreed with us about the same questions. We even told them what the other views were. Still, we had our views and so far as we were concerned, they were right. If we were mistaken it wasn't because we hadn't given it a lot of thought.

Perhaps you're thinking this is a great idea but

you aren't ready or able to jump into a debate with your kids about some things. Even though you have the right attitude and you're interested in getting your kids into a discussion in which a Christian view is presented, you can't do it yourself.

I say do it anyhow. Try. Do the best you can. Ask them questions about their questions. Don't worry if you don't have all the answers or even some answers. Your kids will respect you for listening and trying. Then after dinner head over to the nearest Christian bookstore and pick up a book or two on the subject and read it word for word, even if you can't understand it all.

You can talk to your pastor. Most of the time he can help. If he can't, he can guide you to someone who can. You may even have an unofficial resident theologian or two in your church (every church has at least one). Take them to lunch or coffee and pick their brains.

You have other options too. You can find Christian videos on almost any subject by America's best evangelical thinkers. Sit around and watch them with your kids. Then talk about them. Take your kids to seminars, debates, lectures. If there's not one in your town, pick a weekend, pack the family in the car and head for the big city to hear some speaker or listen to some debate. It's great family fun and it will mix some very happy memories with some very serious experiences. That combination can have far-reaching consequences for spiritual good.

When our daughter was a junior in high school, I took her to a debate between a local college professor who claimed to be an atheist and the brilliant, young Christian philosopher and author Dr. J. P. Moreland.[1] The subject was, "Is There a God?" and the dialogue that ensued between these two intelligent, learned men that evening was nothing less than magnificent.

Of course, I thought Dr. Moreland won the debate (can you guess why?) and as I was driving home I spoke enthusiastically to my daughter about the evening.

"Tina, that was the real thing," I said excitedly. "That was a defense of our faith and our belief in God in the finest manner possible. It won't get any better than what you heard tonight."

Tina, who is usually the enthusiastic one in our family, seemed quiet and subdued. She spoke softly but with conviction.

"Dad, that was incredible," she replied, shaking her head slowly. "I had no idea you could talk about Christianity that way. I just wish some of my friends could have heard it."

Dr. Moreland's thinking faith had scored a direct hit. In two hours he had made an indelible impression on an impressionable young woman who was serious about her faith. I knew those two hours were an investment of my time that would pay large, eternal dividends over the course of her lifetime.

Friends, hear the good news: Ours is a God of evidences and explanations. He is there and He has made Himself known. We can answer the faith-related questions asked by our children and our friends. Believing the gospel is not a leap in the dark.

Yes, it is true that we must beware of the dangers of an over-intellectualized faith. When we get to the bottom line we need grasp only one simple truth by faith—Jesus Christ died for our sins. We must repent and believe in Him to find salvation. Nothing else will save us.

But we must also beware of the dangers of an unthinking faith. We cannot expect our children or anyone else who looks to us for guidance to embrace a faith that requires you to check your brain at the door. It won't work.

If you want spiritually strong Christian kids, be certain that thinking hard thoughts about your beliefs is an integral part of the Christian faith you are trying to pass on.

4

Demas and Susan

The best known dropout of all time is the Prodigal Son. Wherever the Bible is read, the story of the rebellious boy and his loving father is known. It's a tender, compelling story.

But for me, the really fascinating New Testament story of faith rejection is Demas, one of Paul's disciples. "Demas has forsaken me," Paul records simply in 2 Timothy 4:10, "having loved this present world, and has departed for Thessalonica."

We don't get any more information about Demas here than this brief, poignant comment. However, we can piece his story together from some other New Testament references and get some idea of what happened. Come along and meet this lesser known prodigal.

We know first of all that Demas was not a quickie believer who never quite got his feet on the ground spiritually. In Philemon 24 (NKJV), Paul describes Demas as a "fellow-laborer," a compliment by any standard of judgment. No one got listed as a fellow-laborer of the apostle Paul because he was into religious games.

By putting together a chronology based on the three references to Demas, we know that he worked with Paul for probably three to five years which suggests that he was a pretty serious Christian. Demas knew exactly what the Christian faith was about and precisely what Paul was trying to accomplish on his missionary journeys.

But something else was going on inside this young man. Somewhere along the way, his faith had begun to unravel. When everything finally came loose, he made the move he had no doubt been contemplating for a long time. He bailed out. Took off for the city lights.

I'd give a week's salary to know what was going through his mind in the weeks before he departed for Thessalonica. I'd give even more to know what he felt, to sense something of the emotions that tore at his heart and soul as he moved toward the big decision. It couldn't have been easy.

Paul's explanation is simply that Demas "loved this present world" and "departed." But that seems to be more the result than the cause. My question is why did he change his mind about what was important? What was going on in his life that made Thessalonica and this present world more attractive than Jesus Christ and serving God? One does not simply decide one day to give up following the Lord. It takes time and trouble to make a U-turn like that possible.

Does Paul know more than he is telling us? Or is his comment about Demas the logical conclusion about someone who takes off unexpectedly? We don't know with certainty. But if you will give me a little room to maneuver, I'd like to surmise a bit about this story.

A Few Educated Guesses About Demas

At bottom, I think Demas was a disillusioned Christian. I think he lost heart. He tried. Gave it all he had but in the end it wasn't working for him. Somehow what he believed and what he experienced became separated. Mix in the difficult circumstances of Paul's final imprisonment and you have a recipe for emotional and spiritual discouragement that turned into a decision to leave.

Where had Demas come from? Were his parents believers who had opened their home to Paul on one of his missionary journeys? Can we picture Demas, young and impressionable, sitting at the dinner table fascinated by the dynamic apostle and his go-go-gospel? Fired up, he offered to help Paul in any way he could just so long as he could be with him.

Or was Demas a convert as an adult? At some point along the way, possibly on a busy street corner in a bustling city, he may have lingered at the edge of a crowd listening to Paul speak persuasively about the glorious salvation that is in Christ Jesus. Something clicked. This was what he was searching for! This was *the* answer. He would follow Jesus and he was sure the best way to do that was to be with this fascinating man Paul.

Demas did well for quite a while. He threw himself into the ministry. Gave it his all. But then things started to turn sour. Even though he had dedicated himself to God, he began to realize that this Christian business was harder than he thought. Sometimes his faith didn't seem real. His doubts grew. Disappointments increased. He saw flaws in his fellow Christians—maybe even in the great apostle himself.

Something had happened to his simple, joyful faith. No matter how hard he tried, the fire was dying. He was working zealously but he wasn't feeling much.

Where was the peace of God Paul always talked about? Or the power of God? And prayer? He hadn't prayed, really prayed, in months.

And so at last, he walked away. For one young man in the first century, the record tells all: "Demas ... departed." Apparently, the gospel was not the answer to his questions or the solution to his problems after all.

When we talk about Demas, it's easy to think that the point of the story is that he walked away. And so he did. That is what disturbs us. But the real point of the Demas story is his spiritual disillusionment, his disappointment with God. That is *why* he walked away. If we can understand that aspect of the Demas story, we can learn something that will help us and others who may be as ready to walk away from their faith today as Demas was in his day.

For Demas, the gospel had not lived up to its billing. True, it worked for a couple of years. But then, just when he needed its power, joy and victory the most, it failed him. Or so he surely must have thought. Somehow, the good news had turned into the bad news.

Spiritual meltdown. Faith freefall. Call it what you like, but see the point: You can be intellectually and volitionally committed to serving Christ while at the same time you are emotionally and spiritually far away. When that internal split takes place, dropping out is not far behind.

A Believer Named Susan

The story of Demas has been repeated thousands of times throughout history. People who once followed Christ have become profoundly disappointed in their faith and have decided that they could no longer follow Christ.

Some of these dropouts have become so disillusioned with the Christian faith that they have resorted to almost any means of escaping from it all, including self-destructive behavior. That's what happened to Susan, a young pastor's wife who went from spiritual commitment and an earnest enthusiasm for the Lord's work to spiritual despair and bitterness toward everything related to Christianity. Susan's story is Demas revisited, only with the details.

The oldest of four children born into a conservative, evangelical Christian home, Susan was a pleasant, cooperative young woman whose first instinct was to smile when she talked to people. When someone at church needed help they asked Susan first because they knew she would say yes. Susan couldn't say no to anyone, especially Jesus Christ.

Somewhere early in her life Susan decided to dedicate herself entirely to the Lord. Was it a church altar call or a camp fire meeting complete with sticks to symbolize your life cast into the flames of God's consuming love? She couldn't remember exactly, but she knew what she knew: She would be whatever God wanted her to be, whether it was a missionary, a Christian worker or anything else. What and where were not issues.

During her difficult teenage years in high school, Susan remained faithful to her Christian commitment. Sometimes she carried her Bible on top of her books as a "witness" to her Christian beliefs and values. Once she took her guitar to school and sat on the front steps after classes and sang Christian songs. Talk about peer pressure! Can anyone *not* appreciate her courage and spiritual determination?

Susan met Bill when she was a junior in Bible college. Bill was a nice looking, personable young man who was preparing for the pastoral ministry. Part of his preparation plan included finding a good Christian wife—like Susan.

By her senior year, Susan was certain her calling in life was to be a pastor's wife—Pastor Bill's wife, to be exact. Things were happening just as she had hoped and prayed.

Bill and Susan were married in the fall following their graduation. In November, Bill received a call to a small church in the southeastern United States. Her dream had become a reality. Ten years later it would become a nightmare.

Bill's first two pastorates were relatively successful. Church attendance improved, annual giving increased and Bill became an increasingly effective speaker whose preaching talents were becoming noticed in wider circles.

Then came the call to a large, urban church where Bill's many gifts could be fully utilized. This church also prospered under Bill's capable leadership. It was a case of his first two churches to the tenth power. Bill became one of the area's better known pastors and was invited to speak at various services and functions.

One of the hidden reasons Bill's pastorates were so successful was Susan. She was everywhere, giving her time and talents without regard to herself. Just as she had done when she was a little girl, she helped wherever she was needed, including the church office where she did clerical work and answered the phone when the part-time paid secretary was not there. In their first church she played the piano for every service. Later, she would fill in when asked. Susan was the ideal pastor's wife.

Turmoil Beneath the Surface

On the surface it was perfect. Successful pastor and good husband; supportive pastor's wife and good mother. But underneath Susan's pleasant exterior things weren't going as well. At times, she found herself asking why the church paid someone to play the organ but would not pay her when she substituted at the organ. The same was true of her work in the church office.

As Bill began to spend more time away from home in speaking engagements, Susan found herself wondering why she too couldn't have a little time off from the pressures of being a wife, mother, Sunday school teacher, unpaid organist, pianist, church secretary and general go-fer.

When Bill came home from his meetings excited about what God was doing, he seemed not to notice her hard work during his absence. Nor did he seem aware of her growing loneliness even though she was in the middle of a busy church situation.

Several times Susan went through spells of depression that lasted several days. She tried on occasions to speak to Bill about these dark moments, but he discounted her comments by saying she would feel better when she got some rest.

No one else was listening either. One time she spoke vaguely of her feelings to a guest speaker at the church. He seemed mildly surprised and suggested that if she were able to spend more time in prayer and Bible study things would surely improve.

Increasingly, Susan found herself wanting to say "no" when asked to do something for the church. Still, she consented to do what she was asked, not wishing to burden others with her troubles. Above all, she did not want to let Bill down or add unnecessarily to his concerns. At times, when she just wanted to get away from the church and its demands, she would go out, get into her car and drive around aimlessly.

Susan knew something was wrong but she didn't know what it was. And she was certain as well that whatever it was, it must be her fault. She was angry when she was supposed to be happy. She was nervous and agitated when she was supposed to be peaceful and contented. She was beginning to question things when she was supposed to be walking by faith. And she was finding her personal devotional life increasingly unfulfilling no matter how hard she tried to make it a vital, meaningful part of her life.

A lovely Christian woman was disintegrating before the eyes of everyone around her and no one saw it happening. A dedicated Christian woman who once desired only to serve God was becoming increasingly confused and disappointed about her service to God and the results that a life of devotion were supposed to produce for her.

Do you know the rest of Susan's story? Can you guess? Susan got involved with another man in the church. It started innocently enough, but before long she was part of a tangled, ugly affair that blasted her and Bill out of the church and almost ended their marriage.

Today Susan and Bill are trying to put their lives back together. It isn't easy. Even with the love of family and Christian friends, as well as professional Christian counselors, their hurt is deep and their difficulties complex. Bill is out of the pastoral ministry, at least for the present, though he hopes to return some day.

Disillusioned about the Christian faith, Susan is barely able to talk about God. She attends church with her family, but does little more than go through the motions. "If the people at church knew what I was really thinking about them and the church," she says while shaking her head, "they wouldn't even associate with me."

You don't need a degree in psychology or theology to understand that Susan is on the edge of giving up her faith in God. Like Demas, she's seen and heard it all and it's not working anymore. She's looking for answers to her confusion and pain, wondering what the future holds in the coming weeks and months. Does it hold faith failure? Spiritual renewal? I give her credit for hanging in there, for still trying.

Maybe you know her. Maybe you can help her find the way.

● ● ● ● ● ● ● ● ● ● ● ● ● ● ● ● ● ● ● ●

5

A Faith That Works

Can someone like Susan be helped? Would she even listen, never mind contemplate a return to a faith experience that had become so negative and life shattering?

People who leave the Christian faith a little later in life are among the hardest of all to help from a spiritual standpoint. Like someone who was ill and took medicine that didn't work, they find it exceedingly difficult to even consider trying the same prescription again.

The good news is that these hurting, disillusioned Christians do not need the same prescription. They can find saving grace without going "back." They can go forward to a new, clearer understanding of God and the Christian life.

We who are strong and whole must help them. We must be the ones who wisely and graciously communicate this "new" understanding of the gospel to those

59

who are spiritually disillusioned. If we don't help them, who will? The only question that remains is how can we help them? What must we say and do?

We who are spiritually whole and strong must say and do at least two things.

First, we must become more open and honest regarding ourselves and our Christian experience. We must stop pretending and start telling the truth. Absolutely and irrevocably, let the religious games end.

Second, we must support this honesty policy by incarnating God's truth and love in authentic Christian lives. We must not only teach these troubled souls that the gospel is true; we must demonstrate that the gospel works. In the final analysis, *that* is what disillusioned Christians do not believe. To reach them, they must see the gospel working in us.

Does it sound too simple? I agree that it does. But I assure you that if we get hold of these two basic elements, we will, at the very *least*, be in a position to intersect spiritual disillusion before it gets a firm hold in the lives of those we love. And if we do these things well, we will, at the very *best*, put an end to faith failures rooted in spiritual disillusion.

Refreshing Honesty

First, honesty and openness.

Would it surprise you if I said I thought evangelical Christianity had an honesty problem? Not doctrinal or biblical honesty. We do pretty well there. We're the Bible-truth people and while sometimes we can be less than exemplary when it comes to honesty in our everyday Christian lives, we typically don't play games with the great doctrines of our faith.

Our honesty problems are more in the area of pretending about our thoughts and feelings, especially as they relate to our faith. We wear what Chuck Swindoll calls psychological "masks."[1] We have an ideal Christian in mind for ourselves, and we go through life trying to be that person, even if it means pretending to be him or her.

Swindoll says our masks are many. We cover our temptation struggles with an "I'm holy" mask. We pretend to be strong so our emotional weaknesses will go undetected by our fellow Christians. We avoid self-disclosure; we hide from ourselves and others. We play every imaginable emotional game, all in the name of appearing to be mature, spiritual Christians.

The trouble with this pretense is that it fools the very people who need our honesty the most: the disillusioned, the strugglers, the wavering. Painfully aware of their own uncertainty and confusion, our "weak in the faith" brothers and sisters see our smooth spiritual masks and conclude that they aren't even close to being that kind of Christian. Discouraged by their dismal performance, they wonder what is wrong with them.

One young man I interviewed spoke quietly of his longing to know his minister father as a real person rather than the victorious spiritual leader he always appeared to be. It was not that he disliked his father's ideal Christianity or even criticized him for being so "straight" in his lifestyle and everyday demeanor. It was that his father did not seem to be a real human being.

"I never heard my father say, 'Wow, what a nice-looking woman,' " he sighed with an unbelieving look on his face. "I don't know whether or not my father ever *looked* at other women, never mind measured them for a moment. I just wish that he had said to me, 'I'm attracted to a beautiful woman.' He didn't have to say he'd ever contemplated going to bed with one."

As it happened, this young man was involved

sexually with a young woman who attended his father's church. His father, who was the pastor of the church, was unaware of his son's sexual misconduct which was going on even as the father preached passionately to his congregation about the need for purity in the life of every believer.

What this young man did not know was that I knew his father when he was young. Indeed, I knew him well enough to know that he struggled mightily with his sexual desires and was so frightened by a close encounter of the sexual kind while he was in seminary that he determined he must once-for-all win the battle with his sexuality or abandon his call to pastoral ministry.

I admired his integrity and his courage and his iron self-will. He kept women at arm's length at all times, managing to offend more than a few women in his church by seeming aloof and cold. Today he is a respected pastor and a man of great spiritual passion to whom others look for Christian leadership. He was and is what people call a "winner."

But there is one sense in which he is losing the battle. His plaster-mold perfection is a kind of dishonesty that disserves people who look to him for spiritual leadership. To some, he appears unhuman and saint-like. His Christianity seems beyond them. Yet the truth is he is a human being like other human beings. He knows that young men wrestle with sexual temptation. Instead of pretending that he never felt a surge of desire toward a woman (or pride, anger, jealousy, bitterness, anxiety), would it not be better to admit to his son and to others that he is a man and that only by God's grace is he able to keep himself from caving in to the weaknesses of the flesh?

Some will disagree at this point, noting that such a strong display of personal purity and spiritual strength in a Christian leader could only pull others upward.

Why let people down by telling them about your weaknesses? After all, isn't there a desperate need for spiritual role models with high standards in the ministry these days?

No doubt about it. I'd rather have the father's purity than the son's sin. But how much better to have the father's discipline and high standards along with a heart of honesty that admits struggling with self and sin. How much more real and true his faith would be to all who knew him if only he would bare his soul from time to time. Discretion yes, but heart honesty also!

This kind of truth telling doesn't let people down. Rather, it lifts them up. It sets them free and gives them hope. Instead of thinking they can never measure up, it helps them realize that people who live effective and joyful Christian lives do so in spite of their weaknesses and shortcomings. It helps them put flesh and blood on Paul's confident assertion that he could "do all things through Christ" who gave him strength (Philippians 4:13). In the end, it rids them of illusions about how their problems will go away when they become believers. Knowing this, they will not be so easily disillusioned.

Jesus said, "You shall know the truth, and the truth shall make you free" (John 8:32). We know He was speaking first about Himself as The Way, The Truth and The Life. But He was also talking about the inward truth that sets people free from their fears and anxieties and disillusion.

King David, who had his own problems with openness and inner truthfulness, came at last to understand that what God wanted from him was "honesty from the heart; yes, utter sincerity and truthfulness" (Psalm 51:6, TLB). And what is truth's reward? A clean heart, joy, right desires and words of praise to God (verses 10-15). You can't get much closer to the goal than that.

Simple honesty. How spiritually freeing and refreshing heart truth is! It rips off our masks and makes us real people who can help others who are struggling spiritually.

Christianity Incarnate

The second way in which we can help people who are spiritually disillusioned is to turn the gospel into words and actions.

What troubles spiritually disillusioned people is not theological orthodoxy. It's orthopraxy. They don't believe that Christianity works. They may have believed that it worked at one time in their lives, but today they don't. Church and the doctrines of the faith are irrelevant. Christian fellowship means little or nothing to them. The Bible is seldom if ever opened. Now they must read the living Word in us.

Incarnation.

Albert, a middle-aged African-American man, sat in my office after work one day and told me the incredible story of his life. Born and reared in a Christian home on Maryland's eastern shore, he decided as a teenager that Jesus Christ wasn't up to the hard problems of life. The gospel was useless when it came to racial hatred and social injustice. Sneering at the naiveté of Christianity in the real world, he turned and walked away from the faith of his home and church.

Incited to personal and social violence by H. Rap Brown, Al rampaged his way through life until one day he looked up and found himself behind bars, his life in ruins. With nothing left but time to do, he found himself thinking about the God of his home and church.

Slowly but surely he found his way back to the

faith he had once rejected. A little New Testament, given to him by a friend, guided his steps to the Savior and a total dedication of his life to Jesus Christ. He served his time and never looked back. Today he is a spiritual leader in his church and is studying for full-time Christian ministry.

As I listened to Al's story, I wondered what had made him begin thinking again about God and Jesus Christ. Was he not convinced long ago that faith in Christ was no answer? Why did he even turn around and look back at his childhood faith?

When I posed these questions, Al sat for a moment with his chin resting between his thumb and forefinger and said nothing.

I could see from the expression on his face that he had not thought about his journey back to the Lord in those terms.

He gazed at the ceiling for a moment then looked at me with a sense of self-revelation and said, "I think it was my mother's love." He went on to say with feeling that he knew that "no matter what happened, no matter what I did or where I was, my mother loved me."

The Word made flesh. No sermon or Scripture text could reach this hurting and disillusioned young man caught up in his rage against the world. He was blind and deaf to the gospel, however clearly he heard it taught in Sunday school and preached in church. What reached and held him—what he couldn't forget or ignore—was Calvary's love reflected through the prism of his mother's love.

In his book *Peace Child*, missions strategist Don Richardson explores the idea that the gospel can be communicated by what he calls "redemptive analogies." Even if one knows a tribal language, Richardson says, conceptual barriers can block a clear understanding of the God of the Bible. By using local customs, symbols and words, a missionary can make analogies to the great truths of the gospel and thereby make God's redeeming love known to all mankind.

A mother's love is a redemptive analogy. I am certain as well that parental love is a universal redemptive analogy. Surely it is one of the "witnesses" Paul says God has given of Himself to all people (Acts 14:17). Everyone has a mother and father whose most basic instinct is to love their children. When we love our children, they see a reflection of the great creator/redeemer God who loves them and gave His Son to save them from their sins.

Ruth and Billy Graham, who are perhaps the world's best-known Christian parents, showed their children the redeeming power of parental love. In her book, *Prodigals and Those Who Love Them,* Ruth Graham shares some of her feelings as a mother who knew the pain and sorrow of sons who wandered far from God. The joyful part of her story is not only that her sons came back to God, but also that they gave themselves to the Lord in full-time ministry.

Not long after her book came out, a news reporter asked their son Ned, who is now the pastor of a church in Auburn, Washington, what really happened. Ned replied that he became "infatuated with the drug subculture of the '60s," smoked a lot of pot, used hallucinogens and drank a lot. Then came this telling comment. He said his parents disapproved of his drug use, but never condemned him. In his parents' home, he said, there was an unconditional love "that was irresistible."[2]

At the beginning of this chapter I said that the Prodigal Son of the New Testament is the world's best-known dropout. And so he is. This nameless but famous young man is remembered not so much because he left home, blew his inheritance and ate pig food (a nice Jewish boy, no less), but because his father forgave him and welcomed him back in spite of it all. In every time and culture, people understand love and forgiveness. Yes, you can go home again.

Over the years the father's forgiving love has been the focal point of this story. And it should be since the story is about being lost and found, about sin and salvation. Ultimately, it is a story about the heavenly Father's love for lost sinners and the welcome that awaits all who come to Him.

Correct as it is, this emphasis on the father's forgiveness has obscured an interesting question about the Prodigal Son: Why was he certain he could go home to his father's house? We know what prompted him to consider going home: hunger, destitution and survival itself. But he had burned his bridges. Why did he think that despite everything that had happened, he could go home even as a servant? It was because he knew that his father loved him.

When the Prodigal Son gathered his goods and money together on that fateful day and left home for a faraway land, he knew in the secret places of his soul that this was not The End. As much as he wanted to get away from his family and do his own thing, he knew something else: He was loved. He could go home again. It was probably the only thing about life that he knew for certain.

Parental love tells our children in an unmistakable language that God is love. The same is true of all the lovely graces of the Christian life. Every human being understands the universal language of kindness, patience, gentleness, understanding and acceptance. How lovely and winsome and true these appear to people who have given up hoping in the gospel.

It's not an easy thing to offer these gracious gifts to a hostile, rebellious child or an angry, cynical friend.

Our own hurt and disillusionment are a more natural response to those who reject us and our God. Still, like Albert's mother, and Ruth and Billy Graham, and the Prodigal Son's father, we must show and tell our children and friends a living gospel they can neither deny nor forget.

A Word of Encouragement

At this point you may be thinking about Demas and the apostle Paul. What about redemptive analogies there? Isn't it a little confusing to talk about living out the gospel as an antidote to spiritual disillusion when Demas walked away after working with one of the greatest Christians ever?

If nothing else, the Demas story, short and sad as it is, teaches us that we cannot always help others. We will not always be able to pass our faith on to our children or dissuade our friends from walking away from their Christian faith or persuade them to come back. All we can do is try.

Parents of prodigals, be comforted. You can't get any better at teaching the faith than the apostle Paul. Demas knew God's truth. He understood the gospel. Friends of faith dropouts, be encouraged. You can't live a more consistent, more dynamic Christian life than Paul. Demas saw the gospel incarnated daily. If one of Paul's closest companions can walk away from the Christian faith, anyone can.

One final thought about Demas and then I am done. Remember that Demas is only part of the story. Indeed, he is the exception. In the verses that follow, Paul tells us the rest of the story: Crescens, Titus, Luke, Mark, Tychicus, Carpus, Priscilla, Aquila, Onesiphorus, Erastus, Trophimus, Eubulus, Pudens, Linus, Claudia. Remember them? They're the ones who stayed along with the "all the others" (2 Timothy 4:21 TLB).

And then there is Paul himself. He finished the race. He remained faithful to God. "I have kept the faith," he says in 1 Timothy 4:8, as if to answer the Demas question that is probably weighing on his mind even as he writes these words.

Paul knows in *whom* he has believed. He knows, too, that "finally, there is laid up for me the crown of righteousness, which the Lord, the righteous Judge, will give me on that Day, and not to me only, but to all who have loved His appearing" (verse 8).

When all is said and done, we must understand that each person decides his or her own spiritual destiny. All our efforts, good as they are, must ultimately give place to simple faith in a faithful God. He alone is able to deliver us and our children.

Those who walk away must also reckon with Jesus Christ. However hostile or embittered they may be, however hurt or confused they feel, Christ alone holds the key to their lives and their spiritual disillusion.

6

Bill

Baltimore is a great seafood town. Fresh fish, succulent oysters and delicious crabs pour into area restaurants from the Chesapeake Bay, a beautiful body of water H. L. Mencken once described as nature's protein factory.

To Marylanders, crabs are a delicacy. To outsiders, crabs look grotesque. One minister friend, called to a Baltimore area church from a pastorate in the South, fled nauseated from his church's first outdoor crab feast. He returned a half-hour later looking sheepish and carrying a large box of Kentucky Fried Chicken. No crabs for him, thank you.

Fresh oysters on the half shell look even worse. For those who have never indulged, eating a raw oyster is the ultimate test of moral courage. Guests of mine (grown men, no less) have tried, but upon seeing the gourmet delight lying open before them, refused to go through with it. One out-of-town friend lamely excused himself by insisting that oysters were "too aesthetically deprived to be served as food."

For seafood lovers like myself, Baltimore's Lexington Market is the place to go. Located several blocks from the downtown business district, this wonderful assortment of bakeries, fruit, fish and meat stands is a holdover from an earlier open-air farmer's market, only this one has a roof over it. Here, among crowds of shoppers and business as usual, one can momentarily forget the problems of life and the burdens of the day while consuming a half-dozen freshly shucked oysters over the counter at Faidley's.

Bill and I met for lunch at Lexington Market. It was a beautiful October day. The air was crisp, the sky was clear (for a change) and the trees were bursting with color. The market was humming with noontime activity: business men and women grabbing a quick lunch, housewives shopping, visitors sightseeing, folks just hanging out. Marvelous fragrances met us at the door: Greek gyros, baked goods, fried chicken, seafood, chocolates.

Faidley's was our first stop. We knew what all Baltimoreans know: Newly harvested Chesapeake Bay oysters are always available at Faidley's in all months that contain the letter "r." Oysters on the half shell at Faidley's. Friends, this is living.

We both downed a half-dozen oysters then went around the corner and down the aisle to Lentz's where we ordered two cups of crab soup and two crab cakes on crackers. Seafood treats in hand, we wound our way through the bustling crowd and up the stairs to an open, balcony-like area where we claimed one of the round, spindle-legged tables overlooking the southwestern side of the market.

Bill had something on his mind. A month earlier, he had invited me to lunch at an exclusive downtown restaurant. I went. Lunch on Bill seemed like the perfect remedy for a slow day in the office. Plus, as casual friends, a pleasant lunch would provide the ideal opportunity for us to get better acquainted.

The food was exquisite and the service even better. We chatted about various things, none important. Bill made some comments about the Christian faith that at the time seemed curious to me but not enough to prompt a serious discussion. I added a thought or two to what he said and went on. In sum, it was a pleasant, relaxing time, at least for me.

Afterwards, I wondered why Bill had invited me to lunch. Perhaps that is an indictment of modern-day relationships or possibly of me for thinking there must be some reason for Bill to take me to lunch, other than looking for a way to blow $35. That's pushing casual friendship a little too far, right?

When Bill called two weeks later and invited me to lunch again, I knew something was up. I guessed that the first lunch was a preparation for this one. What Bill had in mind but did not say on that occasion, he would say this time around. I realized too that during lunch number one Bill was testing me, watching my response to his comments while trying to get a reading on how I might react if he unloaded some stronger stuff. I was certain he would let it all go this time.

Bill is a Christian. His father is not a preacher, but was (and is) very active in church. So Bill practically grew up in church like some kind of variant PK only without the title. Sunday school, church services morning and evening, young people's meetings and even some Wednesday evening prayer meetings were an integral part of his childhood. Christian clubs at school, summer camp and retreats too.

Bill is a businessman. In less than ten years, he took a medium-size family business and built it into a large multi-faceted corporation. He is known and respected in the business community for his entrepreneurial creativity and aggressiveness, but even more for his ability to make money. People know Bill because Bill knows money.

If you follow Bill around for a week, you will soon discover that he has all the gadgets that signify success in America: a big home on the water, fancy foreign-made cars, a boat, exotic vacations, money to burn. Bill's life was the American dream come true.

Bill's Drift Away From the Faith

I say "was" purposely, because on this lovely day in October amid the noise and bustle of Lexington Market, these "toys" of the good life were meaningless to a Christian man whose life was coming apart. Bill had problems that were too big for his creativity to solve or his money to fix. He was in trouble and he knew it. He knew, as well, that if he didn't do something soon, his problems would destroy him and his family and probably his business as well.

"You know I'm up to something, don't you," Bill asked with a trace of a smile as he sat down opposite me. "First Tio's and now Lexington Market." He paused, still reading me a little. "Well, I am."

Bill looked both ways, as if expecting someone to be listening or watching. Satisfied with the noise and hubbub (and, I presume, the absence of recognizable faces), he looked at me and said simply, "I've got myself in a mess, Tom. I've got to do something, but first I need some perspective."

Bill wasn't smiling anymore. His face had taken on a flat look and he was becoming slightly flushed. I nodded a little, trying to affirm his freedom and safety. To the crowd around us, I'm sure we looked like a couple of guys talking business. And we were. Serious business.

"To begin with," Bill said in a direct way, "I'm this far from falling in love with another woman." He held up his thumb and forefinger about an inch apart. "I haven't been to bed with her yet, but I'm thinking about it."

I said nothing, but I made a little "Hmm" sound. I wrinkled my forehead and shook my head slightly from side to side.

Bill kept talking. "And if that's not enough," he said a little more intensely, "my Christian life is zero. Zilch."

The words were coming rapid fire now.

"I'm playing at church. I sit in the pew on Sunday morning and my mind is a million miles away. I don't hear anything. I don't feel anything. The truth is, I'd rather be golfing. Really. I'd rather be out on the links and there I am sitting in church with my wife as if it were the most important thing in my life."

Bill stopped momentarily, looked down at his half-eaten crab cake and shook his head. Then he looked up.

"Know why I want to talk about it? I woke up in the middle of the night a couple of weeks ago. My heart was beating like I was running a 10K race. Talk about scared. I started praying for God to help me. I was sure I was having a heart attack."

Bill paused momentarily and gave me a wondering look.

"And would you believe, my heart slowed down to normal? I laid there for a couple of minutes, sweating and wondering what was going on. I couldn't go back to sleep. Then I thought to myself. 'You lousy hypocrite. You never pray anymore and now you've got foxhole religion when your heart starts racing in the middle of the night.' I knew that night God was trying to get my attention."

I said nothing for a moment, then spoke quietly.

"I hear you, Bill. I appreciate your honesty and your desire to get things turned around. I hope I can help."

I knew this was not the time to judge or condemn. Somewhere along the way, someone, probably his pastor, would have to confront Bill about his sin and his spiritual failure. Bill would have to face it all honestly and openly and let God do His breaking, cleansing and healing work. That process would be a necessary part of Bill's journey back to spiritual wholeness. But not now. This was the time for grace and understanding. And besides, Bill had asked me for perspective, not judgment.

I agreed that God was indeed trying to get his attention. What an astonishing story about the racing heart. What an awesome God! What other deity in this mad world would care enough about a wandering soul to seek him in his sleep?

Surely God had been calling Bill day after day, trying to get his attention, trying to catch his eye. But Bill wasn't looking or listening. He saw nothing. He heard nothing. Then came the racing-heart episode like the Old Testament call of God to the boy Samuel. And in that frightening encounter with his own mortality, Bill heard the voice of God. At last he knew that he must go face to face with the true and living God.

Bill and I talked for a hour or so, much to the disappointment (and probably fury) of hungry lunchers looking for a place to sit. Bill had asked for my perspective, and in the course of our conversation, I offered him two angles of vision.

One: For him to continue to be involved in any way with another woman was playing with fire. A disaster already happening. On that issue, he had no options. He had to end that relationship and find ways to ensure it stayed ended. That, or risk a personal tragedy, not to mention the wrath of the same God who had waked him so definitively in the night hours.

Two: He was playing a mind game with his faith. Maybe he didn't think of it that way. But really, he was kidding himself. Possibly it was worse. More like pretense. Or deception. The sooner he faced that reality, the sooner he would come to grips with his sin and spiritual failure. I said something I'm sure Bill did not expect.

"If you hate church so much, Bill, why don't you just stop going? Why not stick your clubs in the trunk on Sunday morning, drop your wife off at church and head for the golf course?"

My suggestion did not sit well with Bill. Why not? Because he thought of himself as a Christian who believed the Bible, someone who was going to church and who was a good-standing member of the community of faith. For Bill, playing golf at 11 A.M. on Sunday morning would be crossing the Rubicon. Making the move. Getting out.

"I couldn't do it," he said abruptly, obviously agitated by my suggestion.

"Why not?"

"Because it's important for me to be in church on Sunday. I may talk about golfing during church but that's nothing more than a state of mind. I don't want that to happen. Besides, I don't doubt my faith. I'm just burned out spiritually or something."

I had no intention of pushing my point. My purpose was not to get Bill out of church but to get him to confront the issue, to see the game he was playing along with its implications. Bill had said with conviction at the beginning of our conversation that he would rather be on the golf course than in church. Were those just words popping out of his mouth without meaning? Dreamtalk? Or was he speaking from the "abundance of the heart" in the manner Jesus described in Matthew 12:34 when He explained how you can really know someone? Words and hearts are vitally connected, according to Jesus.

Faced by my direct question, Bill said he wouldn't go golfing at 11 A.M. on Sunday. But in fact, he was already on the golf course.

In terms of spiritual reality, Bill was gone from his church and his faith. What's more, he was very close to being gone from his lovely Christian wife and two teenage children. Only the game in his mind allowed him to believe otherwise. To actually go golfing on Sunday morning would be to tell his wife, his friends—and himself—that he had indeed walked away from the faith of his home and church.

The De-Sacrilezation of Bill's Life

May I ask you a question? How does something like this happen? How does a man who grows up in a Christian home, confesses Jesus Christ as his Savior, worships in a Bible-believing church and sometimes studies the Bible at lunchtime with other Christian businessmen get this far away from God without seeing what is really going on in his life?

You want to know how it happens? By playing games with yourself and God. You start to drift away slowly. Nothing radical or violent. You believe one thing; you do another. Nothing major at first. You go places that damage your soul; you see and do things that deflect you from the upward vision; you compromise your views about God a little. Your personal Bible study and prayer time slips, then slides, then ends. You skip church activities. Bit by bit, you go.

Other things start to loom larger in your life. Business and professional goals get the lion's share of your time and energy. You start moving up life's social and economic ladders, and now you've got new pressures in your life. Problem relationships dominate you. Sexual frustrations overcome you; sexual fantasy follows. Then action. The pressures of real life in the real world slowly but surely push the life of the Spirit into the background. Time pressure. Peer pressure. Performance pressure. It happens to teenagers, college students, business people, in the workplace, at home, with recreation—all of life.

You aren't necessarily angry with God or church. In fact, in your mind, you still basically agree with the Christian view you have always held. Your doctrinal beliefs are intact. You go to church, talk the language, move through the motions. But in reality you've departed from the faith you claim to believe.

Sociologists call what happened to Bill the "desacrilezation" of life. In everyday language this means that life was slowly becoming less religious to Bill. It means that his once "sacred" view had become more secular. Bill was in the process of changing his mind about what was important to him.

For centuries, Christians have called this kind of faith exiting by a different name: backsliding. That may sound a little old-fashioned today, but in fact backsliding is an apt description of this experience. It is sliding back. Slipping. It is drifting away, passively or actively, from the spiritual values and commitments which were once at your vital center. It is taking a hike because the practical pressures and realities of life have become more important to you than spiritual realities.

Many centuries ago, the apostle John talked about followers of Christ losing their first love (Revelation 2). You're a believer and you started out well. You've been active for God, going to church, doing and saying the right things. But "I have this against you," John says, "that you have left your first love" (verse 4). What was once first in your life no longer occupies that place. God is second (or somewhere else) and other things are first.

Exiled and lonely on the island of Patmos, John may have been thinking of friends like that (or someone he himself loved but could not now see) when he used his "first love" metaphor to describe the spiritual problems of the church in Ephesus. They had once loved Christ with the same intensity of two people who fall in love for the first time. Now other things had intruded into the relationship, weakening and finally destroying the passion for God that had once dominated their lives.

Bill had lost his first love for Christ. Yes, he was attending church and going through the routines of the Christian faith, but the real truth is that he was gone. Had he not heeded the call of God that night, it would have been only a matter of time before his life crashed down around him, making his faith departure known to all.

Several days after our Lexington Market lunch, Bill called to tell me he had met with his pastor and an elder and had told them the whole story. Bill openly accepted responsibility for what had happened and repented and confessed his sin to God in prayer together with these spiritual leaders. He had "turned the corner" and was heading in the right direction, he said, including committing himself to a specific series of spiritual disciplines.

Bill had faced the "other woman" issue as well, and was no longer involved with her. This had been harder than he expected but with God's help he was attempting to put that relationship out of his life forever. He was accountable directly to his pastor for this and had agreed to a process of regular discussions with him about the relationship. He added that he knew he must also work on his marriage relationship as part of his commitment to a "new" life.

Wandering away stories don't always work out as well as Bill's. Somehow, in the mystery of God's will, Bill heard the loving call of the seeking Shepherd and knew with certainty that this was his chance to go home. And he went.

7

A Faith That Endures

Prone to wander, Lord, I feel it—
Prone to leave the God I love—
Here's my heart, O take and seal it,
Seal it for Thy courts above.

—George Robertson

Can you relate to Bill? I can.

I understand how someone can play games with God and drift to the edge of spiritual disaster without fully realizing what is happening. When Bill's story started to unfold on the second floor of Lexington Market that fall afternoon, something trembled in me. Know why? Because I sensed the danger in my own life.

Of the four reasons why most people leave the Christian faith, wandering away is the route I'd take. No, I'm not a phony or a religious trickster. I'm a real person trying, striving, reaching for the prize of the high calling of God in Christ Jesus. But I know how easy it is to drift, to say one thing and do another. I know what it means to talk to a group of young couples about the disciplines of the Christian life and then go home, lie down on the couch, watch two hours of sports and stumble to bed without a moment of prayer or meditation in the Scriptures.

I also know that life with its routine pressures and distractions can take me away from the God I love. Jonathan Edwards, the great Puritan preacher and theologian, believed that the daily grind of life itself was dangerous to the soul because it produces spiritual dullness and makes us insensitive to God.[1]

If drifting away from God is a part of life-as-it-is for adult Christians, consider the dangers and difficulties that await our children as they pass through the firestorm of their teenage and young adult years. How much greater are the challenges they face than those faced by the preceding generation! Substance abuse, sexual promiscuity, materialism, peer and status pressure—all are part of the daily regimen for today's young people.

Faced with these realities, today's teenagers are tempted to back away from their Christian commitments, to wander away from the gospel they have learned at home and church. Every day they hear the message and feel the pressure: Ease up. Don't get so serious about religion. Enjoy life. Be realistic.

Just how far removed are adults from the real world of today's teens? Charles Osteen of Gainesville, Florida, has compared the problems of high schools in the decade of the '40s with the decade of the 1990s. See if you can tell the difference . . .

Top Problems in Public School in 1940

1. talking

2. chewing gum

3. making noise

4 running in the halls

5. getting out of line

6. wearing improper clothing

7. not putting paper in the wastebasket

Top Problems in Public School Today

1. drug abuse

2. alcohol abuse

3. pregnancy

4. suicide

5. rape

6. robbery

7. assault/murder

Little wonder that they drift away. What Christian young man or woman wouldn't at least pause to reconsider his or her Christian commitments under these circumstances? To me, the real marvels are those young men and women who, in a society given over to self-absorption and pleasure, willingly give themselves to Jesus Christ. They're out there in middle school and high school, in college and in the work force. Valiant, honorable young men and women living Christian lives in a society stacked against them. They have my deepest respect.

The good news in the midst of this disconcerting look at today's society is that parents can do more than hope and pray that their children will be able to resist the downward pull of their culture. Parents can help their children *not* drift.

I have two suggestions in particular as to how this can be done, although I'm sure there are more. Perhaps you can add to these.

Providing Spiritual Safe Havens

First, parents can deliberately guide their children into spiritual safe havens where they can find refuge from the world around them. These include formal and informal Christian groups, organizations and activities in which faith is encouraged and spiritual resolve is strengthened simply by being with like-minded Christian friends and peers.

No Christian kid can go it alone. At school, he or she needs the reassuring company of Christian friends. Off-campus Christian parachurch organizations such as Young Life and Youth for Christ provide valuable spiritual safe havens as do youth ministries at local churches. Recent changes in Federal law now permit students to form their own Bible study groups using school facilities. This opens the door to both peer encouragement and evangelism.

When our daughter was in public high school, this law was not in effect. However, she became involved in a school show choir in which there were a number of Christians. The choir director, who was also the music teacher, was a Christian as well. Both on and off campus, these young people did things together, talked about their faith and prayed together about the challenge of living as Christians in a public high school.

Sometimes they went to their teacher's apartment after school or following a concert and enjoyed wholesome fun in a context more specifically Christian than school-permitted. What saving grace for these young people! What critical support at a critical juncture in their lives! The positive effects of that informal but strong network of Christian friends can be seen today in the vital Christian lives of those young people. Thanks, music teacher, for your part in our daughter's spiritual well-being then and today.

Christian camps are also spiritual safe havens. A summer or two working at a Christian camp can create spiritual revolutions. Both of our children spent many summers at a Christian camp where their life's priorities were challenged and their spiritual values shaped.

Taking a summer missions trip with other teenagers can also build spiritual strength and determination. How about a summer with Operation Mobilization or Teen Missions? What about a short-term summer visit to a third world country to help build a church or school? Some of the most powerful, soul-searching Christianity our son Jon ever experienced as a teenager was in the mountains of the Dominican Republic with church friends on a summer missions trip. In that country, local believers prayed and believed in a way he had never seen in America. Life-changing scenes! Strong, spiritually energizing experiences!

All of these activities and groups are a necessary part of strengthening the faith of our children. I recommend them and more. If your church doesn't have a youth group, ask if you can start one. If you don't have many young people at your church, encourage your children to go to youth meetings and activities at other churches.

The effect of peer acceptance in church youth groups is in itself a powerful, supportive message. Plan special events for young people in your home. Go places with them. Whatever you can do to keep your children interested in and involved with their faith and their Christian friends will deflect unbelief and lighten their spiritual load.

The Ultimate Spiritual Safe Haven

Along with these vitally important groups and activities, Christian parents can give their children the safe haven of a loving, caring Christian home.[2]

Semanticists tell us that *murmuring* is the most beautiful word in the English language—but they are speaking only of sounds, not meanings. Surely the most beautiful word in the English language is *home*. Mom and Dad. Brothers and sisters. Food and shelter. Refuge and love. Home. It's where we belong, the magnetic north of our deepest feelings, the one place we want to be on the most sacred days of the calendar year and for the most joyful occasions of our lives. It's also the place we want to be when life hurts the most.

Home is God's earthly metaphor of heaven and a precursor of eternity itself. It is the ultimate spiritual safe haven, the first line of defense against the spiritually numbing, hard realities of life. From the very beginning, we must love and care for our children at home so they can survive the gathering storm of peer pressure, thought pressure and social pressure that will be an inescapable part of their lives as teens and young adults.

How do we make our homes spiritual safe havens?

First, by loving our children unconditionally, just as God loves us. By building their self-esteem, spending time with them, doing things with them and talking with them about any subject—including their faith. Some of the best theological discussions we ever had in our home took place in the kitchen over a glass of milk and a peanut butter and jelly sandwich.

Creating spiritual safe havens does not mean our homes must be perfect places where nothing goes wrong. Life doesn't work that way. It simply means our homes should be a secure place where our children know they are safe and loved.

Nor does it mean that we should not discipline our children. Without rules and regulations, home would become a chaotic, unsafe place. The word *discipline* has its roots in the word *disciple:* one who is taught; a learner, a follower. If we want our children to faithfully follow Christ, then wise but firm discipline in the home must be a part of their lives.

Teaching About God and His Truth

Another way we can keep our children from wandering away from the Christian faith is by teaching them about God and the realities of the spiritual world all around them.

I know this is not a very original idea. After all, this is what the church and Christian families have been trying to do for centuries, right? But the sad truth is that most children and teenagers today know very little about the Bible or the God of the Bible. Quiz the average kid in public school about the Bible and you will get a blank stare. My wife teaches music in a public elementary school and when she comes to the spirituals as a part of American music, most of her students have no idea who Moses (of "Go Down Moses") or Joshua (of "Joshua Fit De Battle") are. Incredible!

By the way, kids from Christian homes don't do much better. They might know who Moses and Paul are (don't bet your home on it), but ask them to talk about the Atonement or to name one New Testament prison epistle and they are mute. How about systematic theology and church history? Surely you jest. The terrifying truth is that children even from the best evangelical churches and homes in America are illiterate biblically and theologically.

Now I ask you, if these kids don't know much

about the Bible and God, are there any kids who do? And beyond that scary thought lies another troubling question. How can our children even begin to resist the temptations they face every day if they are not fully aware of what God wants them to do? If their peers pressure them to lighten up on religion, what response will spring to their mind? Will it be rooted in the knowledge of God and the Holy Scriptures? How can our children possibly defend themselves against the hard realities of life if they do not know about the higher realities of God?

In his provocative book, *The Closing of the American Mind,* Professor Alan Bloom says that the Bible is an unknown book in America today. In an earlier time, Bloom says, "Moses and Jesus" had an "imaginative existence" in most people's minds. "Passages from the Psalms and the Gospels echoed in children's minds."[3] What reverberates in the minds of children today are the banal lyrics of the hottest rock star or the empty-headed dialogue of the latest movie or TV program. Unless parents and grandparents, Sunday school teachers and pastors teach them otherwise, the next generation will never know the difference between the secular and the sacred, between time and eternity.

Long before Professor Bloom wrote his best seller, a Christian educator named Frank E. Gaebelein was talking and writing about what he called the "strange biblical illiteracy" of present-day Christians who call themselves "people of the Book."[4] Gaebelein believed that nothing could "revive and reform" the church, not "evangelistic campaigns, liturgy, social action, mysticism, nor charismatic experiences," without a thoroughgoing knowledge of and obedience to the Holy Scriptures.[5]

Teach them! Line upon line, precept upon precept, day in and day out, teach them! From their earliest cognitive moments to the most complex theological or philosophical discussions of their college years, teach them about God and His truth. Teach them who God is, what He has said and what He expects. Withhold nothing. Speak of love, grace, sin, judgment and other God realities until they are fixed in your children's lives and their way of thinking about the world.

I have a friend who attempts to do this teaching creatively so that the knowledge of God becomes synonymous with life's realities. A walk through the woods with his children is merged into a lesson about the majesty of God. A television program about broken families or crack babies becomes a platform for explaining the righteousness of God and the wages of sin. My friend even formulated a theology of trash!

Teach them church history and faith history. In Psalm 44, the writer speaks of the spiritual power of history:

> We have heard with our ears, O God, *our fathers have told us,* the deeds You did in their days, in days of old: You drove out the nations with your hand, but then You planted; You afflicted the peoples, and cast them out. For they did not gain possession of the land by their own sword, nor did their own arm save them; but it was Your right hand, Your arm, and the light of Your countenance, because You favored them (Psalm 44:1-3, emphasis mine).

I have listened with fascination as my father and mother and uncle recounted stories of the great Passaic, New Jersey, revival in the early 1930s. What extraordinary things God did among those young people and what a remarkable ripple effect that awakening has had down to the present day in various ministries, including a major-market Christian FM radio, a Christian camp, a Christian bookstore, and a large church and Christian school in Baltimore. Out of these ministries young people have gone forth to serve Christ throughout the world.

Dr. Richard DeHaan of the Radio Bible Class dedicated his life to the Lord as a child in those New Jersey meetings. That means that the national radio and television ministries of the Radio Bible Class, along with its worldwide literature ministries, are in some measure a part of the aftereffects of the Passaic revival.

Dr. Vernon Grounds, author and former president of Denver Theological Seminary, found Jesus Christ as his personal Savior in that revival. Many years later at Chicago's Moody Church, Dr. Grounds told me that the Passaic awakening was the "greatest movement of God's Spirit" he had witnessed in his lifetime. Spiritual history! Surely the students at Denver Seminary felt some of the reflected light and heat of that experience from Dr. Grounds. Spiritual encouragement and vision are transferred to today's generations in the stories of God's deeds in an earlier generation.

Many individual lives were affected as well, men and women who did not become famous, but who have been faithful servants of Christ in churches and ministries around the country and throughout the world. One of these quiet heroes is my Aunt Henrietta, a great woman of prayer, work and witness who remains active in her local church today at the age of eighty-one.

And so I repeat: Teach your children church history and faith history. One of my fondest childhood memories is of sitting at my mother's knee with my siblings on Sunday afternoons, listening to my mother read stories of great Christians. John G. Paton, David Brainerd, Lottie Moon—I knew you before I knew about Ted Williams or The Lone Ranger. David Livingston and Amy Carmichael—I knew who you were before I ever heard of Joe Louis or Marilyn Monroe. Church history!

If Christian parents don't tell their children about the deeds of God in the lives of His people, no one will. Tell them so they will have spiritually real people and events to draw upon when they need to resist the pulling power of life's hard realities. Tell them so they will know there is a higher reality in life than they read about in school or see on television or hear on the local rock station. Give them real-life Christian heroes after which they can pattern their lives.

But let us not be satisfied with the spiritual *past* when we think about strengthening our children's faith. Let us welcome those strong, wonderful stories and then go on to create our own spiritual present. Nothing influences children more, spiritually speaking, than the demonstration of an authentic Christian faith at home. Even where family relationships are not entirely healthy and where Bible teaching and faith history are limited, a genuine faith lived out with spiritual integrity day after day will remain as a foundation for our children's spiritual stability.

In the end, our personal relationship with the Lord prevents us from wandering as well. Life is always spiritually dangerous. The temptation to walk away never leaves us. We may settle down emotionally and spiritually as we get older, but we remain vulnerable no matter what our age.

However safe we may feel spiritually, our implacable adversary Satan is ready and willing to harm us. The story I told about Bill is what you might expect from a man in middle life, but I can also tell you stories of Christian men and women who messed up their lives in their sixties and even seventies. And who doesn't know at least one story of someone serving God faithfully for most of his or her life only to fall into sin, destroying a ministry and often a marriage and family.

Christian parents today must accept the challenge

of countering the drifting away pull and push of life itself. We must create spiritual safe havens for our
children while at the same time teaching them the God
realities that counterbalance the world realities in
which they live. We must also accept the challenge of
living each day under the spiritual disciplines that will
help us resist the daily downward pull of the world, the
flesh and the devil.

8

Chris

This is the story of Chris, a teenager I met many summers ago at a Christian camp where I was on staff.

Chris was a nice young man, perhaps fifteen or sixteen years old, with a pleasant, easygoing personality. He was witty, friendly and charming, three gifts bequeathed him by his father who was a traveling evangelist and the camp speaker for the week.

I liked Chris from the moment I met him. But I sensed something was troubling this young man. Before the week was over, I knew some but not all of the details. More of Chris's story would come out later. I'll tell you about that in a moment.

When Chris and his dad were at the camp, his father often called him to the front during the evening service to "give his testimony." Chris spoke of his personal faith in Christ with an easy fluency that was entirely believable. Invariably, he concluded his comments by quoting lengthy passages of Scripture in front of hundreds of astonished young onlookers, many of whom had never read the Bible much less heard it recited at length.

At this point I must qualify this glowing description by telling you that Chris had another side. His pleasant demeanor was only half of the picture. For, unknown to those who knew only what they heard in his heartwarming Christian testimony, this young man was also vulgar and profane, especially around teenage girls whom he attracted like flies to a forbidden feast.

In the remarkable way that rumors spread in summer camps, I soon learned that this EK (evangelist's kid) could curse quite as well as he could quote the Bible. His life didn't match his testimony either. Apparently his principle interest when not telling people how much he loved Jesus was to get girls to let him do as much as he could as fast as they would allow it.

When this bit of camp scuttlebutt was confirmed by a second person, I decided to have a friendly chat with Chris.

The next afternoon, I pulled Chris aside and asked him if I could talk with him. He said, "Sure," so confidently, I thought for a moment I had received some faulty information. Surely no one who was so open about his wrongdoing could expect to keep it hidden for long. Why did he seem so unconcerned?

We walked to a lovely picnic area shaded by trees and serenaded by a rippling stream that passed through the center of camp. I sat on one side of an old oak picnic table and he sat on the other.

"Chris," I said in a casual manner, "I've been hearing some pretty nasty stories about you. I hear you're pretty good at cursing and that you're getting rowdy with the ladies. Is it true?"

Chris looked me in the eye and said it wasn't. Everywhere he went, he explained, he had this same problem. Kids were jealous of him and spread lies about him. He had tried to counter these rumors, but people always seemed ready to condemn him. There was nothing he could do about it so he had stopped worrying about it.

Sometimes I can be suckered by a story like this. I like to believe people. Besides, I know from experience that PKs and EKs are held to a higher standard than others and therefore are vulnerable to being quickly accused and readily condemned.

But I knew Chris was lying. He was telling this story as smoothly and believably as he spoke his testimony and quoted Scripture. It wouldn't work. I had two dependable witnesses. For a moment I wanted to confront him with the truth.

Instead, I decided that my question was warning enough. A couple more days and Chris would be gone, traveling on with his father, preparing for the next camp or church, ready to give his testimony and quote the Bible again.

Furthermore, Chris's father almost certainly knew about his son's behavior problems. Maybe that was why Chris was being hauled along on this summer evangelistic tour. It guaranteed that he would be safely surrounded by mostly Christians every day and would hear preaching every night.

I think Chris knew I was on to his game but he said no more. Neither did I. I got up and walked away.

Two nights later, I had one of those strange experiences that stick in your mind for a lifetime.

At the conclusion of the evening service, I was called upon to come up to the platform and lead the song of invitation. It was not my usual responsibility, but I can lead singing, so I went up to help.

As the call to salvation was being extended, the young people in the audience were asked to remain seated with their heads bowed. As I prepared to begin the singing, I looked up and saw Chris immediately. He was sitting halfway back and was not bowing his head or even pretending to pray. He was looking straight at me with a haunted expression on his face.

I couldn't look away from him. It was as if we were talking to each other without words. I could almost hear him asking, "Do you really believe it, Tom? Do you? Are you for real or is this show time again?"

I tried to answer him with my eyes. "Yes, Chris! I do believe. Jesus is for real. Please believe it!"

After a moment that seemed like forever, he looked down and our silent conversation was ended. The next day Chris left with his father and I never saw him again.

Chris's Formidable Challenge

A number of years later a friend told me a bit of news that helped me understand why Chris had tried to live in two worlds that week at camp. This little tidbit of information, which wasn't much more than a passing comment, also helped me understand the incredibly sad look on Chris's face that night when I led the campers in the song of invitation.

Chris had gotten married at age twenty-one and was divorced shortly afterwards. That was startling. But then came the real shocker: Chris's father had arranged the marriage. No, I don't mean he encouraged the couple to get together or that he gave them his blessing. There's ample room for that in Scripture. Chris's father actually arranged the marriage. He selected the girl and arranged for Chris to marry her. And it happened. I found it hard to believe. That kind of thing may take place in other cultures in the twentieth century, but not in America.

Did Chris want to marry her? I don't know. If not, why didn't he just say no or simply run away? Did he see marriage as more of the same game? Or was this an escape, a way out? I don't know.

My friend went on to explain briefly that this was not something new. Chris had been controlled by his father his entire life: behavior, dress, activities, even the way he cut and combed his hair. He didn't know the meaning of the word freedom.

Chris turned his back on Christianity after his marriage ended. He dropped out. I don't know where he is today or whether he has any interest in spiritual things. I hope he does. Indeed, I pray that he is back in fellowship with the Lord and his family.

Yet even with the hopes and prayers of his family and friends, Chris faces a formidable challenge in terms of an authentic faith renewal in his life. Why? Because he has no idea what it means to willingly follow Christ. Despite his testimony about "deciding to follow the Lord," the fact is that he never decided anything. His faith never belonged to him. From the moment he could think and talk, he was squeezed into a mold and made to perform the Christian life. He was told what to do and what not to do, and that's what he did—at least one side of his personality did.

I'll give you another reason Chris will find it hard to consider the claims of Christ upon his life. He doesn't think salvation is real. It may have changed the lives of other teenagers, but it didn't change his. Thoroughly exposed to the virus of law-and-order, do-what-you're-told Christianity, he developed a numbing, deadening immunity to the Real Thing.

A little while back I raised the question of why Chris didn't run away from home rather than get pushed into an arranged marriage. Let me guess: He couldn't. Underneath that pleasant smile and quick wit, Chris was a zombie. He didn't even realize that he had a choice. His only escape in life was to be two people in the same body.

The Need and Right to Choose Christ

I realize that this story is more complicated than I am presenting it. No one gets as tangled up as this young man without the convergence of many events in his life. I also understand that being a teenager is one of life's toughest challenges. Teenagers can do funny things for a while then come back to being normal. But being a typical teenager wasn't what was bothering Chris.

Chris's problems were rooted in his father's determination to control his life. Instead of leading him into spiritual maturity, Chris's father was pushing him away from the Christian faith. By stage managing his son's life, his dad was removing the one element essential to Chris's spiritual authenticity: the need and right to choose Christ and the way of the cross for himself.

True, there is one sense in which Chris "chose" his faith. He did that when he "accepted" the Christianity in which he grew. Unlike some teenagers who rebel outwardly, Chris conformed to the religious requirements of his home and church. But the simple truth is that he did not personally "own" his faith. He never made a real inward decision about that all-important issue.

Although Chris had heard more sermons by the time he was sixteen than most people hear in a lifetime, he had never heard, really heard, the freedom-and-choice words at the center of the gospel: if, come, let, knock, seek, ask, whoever will, whoever confesses, whoever denies. In Chris's mind, Jesus must have been someone who forced you to follow Him, rather than someone who invited you to be His disciple.

Clearly, Chris's dad wanted his son to be a real

Christian, to be a dedicated servant of Jesus Christ. What Christian parents don't want that for their children? All Christian mothers and fathers try to bring their children up to love and serve the Lord.

But instead of letting God do His saving, life-changing work in Chris, this earnest Christian father tried to make something happen. He tried to manufacture a godly son who would be exactly the kind of Christian boy every evangelist hopes and prays for.

I wonder how long Chris's dad knew it wasn't true? When did he know that nothing real was happening in his son's life, spiritually speaking? How much did he know? Was he preaching salvation and holy living night after night, all the while praying that his troubled boy would be the first to respond to the invitation?

How sad that this dedicated evangelist could open his Bible and preach salvation by faith through grace while he practiced hard, uncompromising law in his family. That changed the gospel into a mixed message for his boy. How could Chris fully understand or embrace a faith that invited him to freely make this life-changing decision while at the same time he was never allowed to make any real personal or spiritual decisions?

Fortunately, not many kids grow up in Christian environments as devoid of freedom as Chris's. But you may be sure Chris has "brothers" and "sisters" around the world who are living programmed Christian lives rather than spiritually free lives. These young people may be living correctly in terms of right doctrine, right words, right deeds. Or they may be deliberately living double lives as a means of dealing with their painful, confusing existence.

Whatever their situation, they are living dangerously. Because more than likely they've never made any authentic faith choices. If that's true, they don't have any real ownership of their faith. And that means they're sitting ducks for faith rejection.

● ● ● ● ● ● ● ● ● ● ● ● ● ● ● ● ● ● ●

9

*An Authentic
Faith*

God who made the birds never made bird cages. It is
men who make bird cages, and after a while we become cramped and can do nothing but chirp and
stand on one leg.

—Oswald Chambers

Have you ever lost your freedom?

When I was a student in Chicago in the '60s, I was
arrested by plainclothes policemen while walking to
work in the downtown district called the Loop.

The shock of being apprehended and frisked on a
busy street was bad enough (people are exceedingly
nosey when someone else is in trouble), but being
shoved into a patrol car and whisked off to the police
station was even more humiliating, especially to someone who was studying for the Christian ministry.

But that was just the prelude. When I was taken inside the police station, which looked just like the TV

cops and robbers shows, I was signed in and then put inside a detention area to await my fate. The hour or so I spent inside that cage gave me a brief but completely satisfying look at life behind bars.

I remained relatively calm through all of this until the detectives informed me that the charge against me was murder. At that point I panicked. I had stupidly forgotten to bring my wallet that day so I had no identification, which is why things had gotten this far. Until I was able to establish my identity through a detective's visit to my school, I was left to ponder the prospect of paying the penalty for someone else's sin, something I had only read about in theology books until this moment.

The prospect of losing my freedom for a lifetime was frightening beyond description. The right to be myself, to go or not go where I wished, to speak and act freely without fear of retribution suddenly became more precious to me than I had ever imagined. I did not want to be locked up.

Fortunately, my identification came through. Afterward, when they showed me a picture of the suspect, I saw immediately why they had picked me up. I was a dead ringer for him. The police apologized for the inconvenience and even drove me to the company where I worked a part-time job. No place of employment ever seemed so pleasant.

Freedom. All Americans understand it. We are free. We wouldn't exchange our freedom for any political system or trade it for any material gain, though our radical selfishness and materialism may yet ruin the very freedom we cherish. Still, we know we are free to become as disciplined or decadent as we wish to be.

Christians, like all other Americans, love their freedom. We are quick to defend it because we understand that it allows us to openly practice our faith. We know from history and current events that when governments take away freedom, evangelical believers always suffer.

If this description of Christians as freedom-loving citizens is accurate—and I'm confident it is—we must then ask ourselves a question. Why are Christians so frightened of being free spiritually? Why do we look for someone else to tell us what is right or wrong, instead of being willing to come to our own conclusions through study and prayer?

In addition to this question, we must also ask ourselves why Christians are so unwilling to grant others spiritual freedom, particularly their own children. If an intelligent visitor from another planet were to contemplate the myriad rules and regulations that are part and parcel of most evangelical homes and churches, he or she might well conclude that in these places, freedom is the enemy. This observer might also infer that the right to make an authentic choice in matters of faith is among the most dangerous of all possibilities.

In my interviews with faith dropouts, nothing evoked stronger reactions than the simple question, "Did you feel free to make important decisions about your faith at home and in church?"

Some people used the question as permission to spout off about their homes and churches (did they ever). But most said basically that their parents "expected them to believe." One professional woman in her late thirties told me with exasperation that "doubts and questions never got anywhere in our home. For us it was Christianity—take it or leave it. So I left it."

When Freedom Is Taken Away . . .

Allow me to tell you one freedom-and-choice story in more detail.

Margie was the daughter of missionary parents. When she was in her early thirties, she began to get in touch with some unsettling feelings about her childhood. Why had she been sent away to school as a little girl when her family lived on the mission field? She didn't like being away, nor did she enjoy life at the mission school. It was rigidly disciplinarian, emotionally austere and not at all like being at home with Mom and Dad. Did she have to go through this because her parents loved Jesus?

Still, it wasn't being sent away to school that bothered Margie the most. Slowly but surely she was coming to the realization at this adult stage of her life that she had grown up in an environment in which all of the important choices of her young life had been made by others.

"I absolutely hate my parents," Margie hissed, her gray eyes flashing angrily. "They totally ran my life. I grew up thinking I had to be this perfect little missionary girl who obeyed her parents at all times. And that's what I did. I bought it all—what I thought, how I dressed, what I did, what kind of Christian to be."

Margie paused momentarily and looked me in the eye as if talking to her father or mother.

"But no more," she said almost fiercely, shaking her head side to side. "No more. I'm making my own decisions now. I don't care what they think anymore."

It was no idle threat. Margie is indeed making her own decisions. She has ventured out into a number of freedom-seeking adventures, including finding a new set of friends and activities while distancing herself from the Christian community. She has chosen not to attend church and also refuses to participate in family devotions with her husband and children.

Does she believe she is free at last? I don't know. All I can say is that even as I write this page, Margie's marriage is hanging in the balance. Alcohol is threatening to take total control of her life. Demon Rum imbibed at her own choosing is ruthlessly taking away her freedom of choice—an irony too bitter for words.

Margie's husband has sought help from his pastor but Margie refuses to talk with him. To her, pastors are in a category one step up from the lowest of all—missionaries. Professional counseling and in-patient therapy aren't working either. Margie is as impervious to professional methods as she is to pastors and missionaries.

My heart goes out to this child of the mission field. She is a good but profoundly troubled woman who wants help from no one. God and God alone can save her.

My heart also goes out to Margie's parents. Gentle but strong-minded people, they gave their all to serve Christ in a foreign land. They weren't perfect as parents. Still, they did their best under the difficult circumstances that face every missionary family. Now they must stand by helplessly and watch their beloved daughter come apart personally and spiritually. Helpless is probably the wrong word. They can pray. And I promise you they are praying for their child. May God grant them positive, wonderful answers to the prayerful longings of their hearts.

Praying parents, prodigal child. Is there any way this tragedy might have been averted? I cannot answer that question with certainty, nor can anyone else. But there is little doubt that the prospects for Margie's spiritual well-being would have been greatly improved had her parents allowed and even encouraged her to make her own choices about life and faith.

Certainly Margie's parents meant well. They intended to protect her from making life-damaging mistakes when she was young. But instead, by making all her choices for her, they gave her a hand-me-down faith that became little more than a religious performance on her part. When the rains and strong winds of life blew, Margie's "faith" proved to be little more than a hollow structure that collapsed around her.

In the end, Margie is responsible for her life. She chose and acted, not her parents. But the absence of personal and spiritual freedom in her life increased the likelihood that she would walk away from the Christian faith of her childhood.

The "Sense of Self"

Dr. David Allen, a Christian psychiatrist and the world's leading authority on cocaine addiction and related co-dependency issues, makes an interesting connection between what he calls "the sense of self" and an authentic Christian experience.

"To have a truly meaningful relationship with God," he explains, "we must have some sense of our own identity and individuality." Otherwise, "our faith can become very superficial. We put our identity in the Christian faith and use it as a kind of coping tool. As a result, we never become mature." When this happens, Dr. Allen says, we not only lose the life-giving benefits of a "healthy faith," but we become owners of a "destructive faith."[1]

Guy Greenfield, professor of Christian ethics at Southwestern Baptist Theological Seminary, says that one thing teenagers need and want is the freedom to answer such basic life questions as, "What kind of person will I be? Whom will I choose to relate to on deep and meaningful levels? What is really important in life? What in life has ultimate value? What is the meaning of morality and spirituality?" Professor Greenfield goes on to say that "our children have the right to answer those questions for themselves. We will certainly influence their answers by both words and example, but the final decision is theirs."[2]

Evangelical Christians believe in this kind of freedom and "sense of self" when it comes to personal salvation. We preach with insistence that no one can choose the Savior for us. We teach that a person cannot depend on family, friends, church or anyone else to bring us into a right relationship with God. We alone must decide to accept or reject God's love.

In the same way, we must also believe that freedom and a sense of self are equally important when it comes to living the Christian life. Without authentic choice there can be no authentic faith. Let your children choose! Let them be real Christians and real persons. In so doing, you will increase their faith and decrease the likelihood that they will become faith dropouts.

Becoming Freedom-Granting Parents

How do we become freedom-granting parents?

We begin early but surely. When our children are very young, we make decisions for them. This is our parental responsibility. We know what is right and wrong before they even understand the issues involved. But as they get older, we begin to offer them choices, first in little things, then in larger matters and finally in vital issues of faith and life.

Our daughter Christina attended public schools. When she entered middle school, she was confronted by some new challenges that would soon lead to new choices. Even though she was unsure of herself, she resisted the social pressure of her peers to behave in ways she considered wrong. But it was not long until she began to ask for permission to join in some activities that conflicted with our family values. One of these was school dances.

My wife and I grew up in conservative Christian homes and churches that did not permit dancing. We objected to school dances, even though we knew they were well chaperoned in these grades and were probably not as dangerous or harmful as our upbringing had led us to believe. Still, we thought it best that our children not go.

During one family conversation Tina let us know she was interested in going to the school dance. Here was a test of our conviction that at some point Christian kids must begin to choose for themselves. Should we decide or should our daughter? She clearly wanted to go. We agreed together with Tina that the first time she asked, we would decide. Thereafter, she would have to make her own decision regarding this particular issue.

When the first choice came, we decided no go. Tina accepted our decision, but we could see she was disappointed.

Several weeks later, another dance came up on the school calendar. This time, it was Tina's choice and she decided to go. She was free to choose because of our agreement. And so we let her go even though it made us uneasy.

We tried to treat her decision casually—no grimacing (not easy), no guilt tripping (harder yet), no negative body language. She went and we wondered.

Not too long afterwards, Tina made another decision about school dances. She didn't need to go to these events after all. They weren't for her, at least for now. She might change her mind later (her decision once again), but for the present, she decided not to go. We had deliberately transferred this choice to her, believing she was ready to be her own person regarding this matter. She was free and we were free.

My wife and I attempted to maintain this freedom-granting attitude toward our children throughout their lives. We thought of it as letting out a rope. At first, we had the entire rope in our hands. We held it tightly and firmly. We were in charge and they knew it. But as our kids grew older, we began letting the rope out, deliberately giving them more room to maneuver when we thought they were ready for it. We even told them we were going to let go of the rope one day. What an interesting emotional reversal that little bit of information created in them!

At times, it was difficult for us. Sometimes it was difficult for them. As we look back, we can see that our freedom-granting efforts paid rich dividends. Today, our children are mature young adults who follow Christ because they want to, not because they were manipulated or coerced.

Establishing Freedom That Is Accompanied by Responsibility

It worked for us, but does it always work? What happens when you grant freedom and it results in disaster? How does a parent deal with children who behave unacceptably? What if the freedom you give them results in drinking, drugs and sexual immorality?

In our home, we made it clear that our children were free to choose, but that freedom was accompanied by responsibility. If they chose to behave unacceptably, they would then be responsible to make other choices which are part of the freedom to choose.

For example, if they chose to do drugs (they didn't) or drink (they didn't), the following choice would be to stop or pay the consequence (which in this case would be to find another place to live). They were free, but they could not use that freedom to disrupt our home and family.

Some parents I have talked with about freedom

granting feel it is too dangerous, especially when they have a fourteen- or fifteen-year-old son or daughter who is on the verge of being out of control. One parent in particular, whose adolescent son is actively rebelling against the faith of his home and church, told me flatly he would never give his son more freedom at such a crucial moment in his life. Indeed, he had decided to give his son less freedom and take away some of the independence that was creating the problem.

Most youth experts would agree with this father's determination to stand firm against his son's rebellion. But they would not agree that taking away his freedom is the answer. In fact, they would say that getting more restrictive with a rebelling teenager works against parents.

Robert Dudley, a specialist in youth and faith issues, explains why in an article titled, "Adolescent Heresy: The Rejection of Parental Religious Values."[3] Dudley says that teenage rebellion has its roots in the God-given need of adolescents to separate themselves from their parents. They're trying to discover who they are. Are they an extension of their parents? Of their church? They are asking themselves questions such as, "When will I be old enough for my parents to believe in me? When will they trust me?"

If parents fight this God-instilled desire to become an independent person, they can delay and even damage their child's emotional and spiritual growth. The more parents fight their teenager's need for independence, Dudley says, the more likely it is that adolescents will reject their parents' values. "Religion," Dudley says simply, "can never be passed on by force."[4]

On the other hand, if parents wisely grant their children the freedom they need, they will begin to defuse the potential problems in their children's quest for independence and reduce the threat of faith rejection. Dudley sums up his thoughts this way:

> When adolescents perceive that their parents are not fighting them or trying to thwart their independence, but are listening to them, struggling to see things through their eyes, and helping them reach their goals, much of the pressure to reject parental values is removed.[5]

So now, what if you are a parent who has severely restricted your children and you are beginning to sense that you may need to give them more freedom? Possibly you have teenagers who are fighting you and by extension your faith. Surely you can't just drop one approach and take up another, especially when one seems to contradict the other. What effect would that have on your children?

In a word, probably a good one. The leap to liberty is shorter than you think.

Freedom granting does not require cradle-to-teenager preparation, though that may be the most desirable methodology. Freedom can be granted incrementally even when your children have already reached their teen years. Just shorten the timetable and implement your plan faster. You might begin this way.

Call a family discussion (or slip into one after dinner) and announce that things are going to change in your family. Tell your kids that Mom and Dad have thought and prayed a lot about giving them more freedom to make their own decisions, including the ones they've been fighting about lately.

After your teenagers recover from the shock, you can explain that you have come to see that they need more freedom in order to become themselves and to grow into mature Christian young people who take responsibility for their own lives.

In fact, you realize that the issue that is most important of all—their faith in Christ and obedience to Him—is really a decision they have to make on their own. You've tried to show them the way and maybe you've even tried too hard to make them do what you believe is right. But now, things are going to change and they will have to make those decisions for themselves.

At this point, or perhaps after some discussion (providing your kids have not been rendered speechless), you can announce a Freedom Plan in which you will grant specific freedoms over a period of time from the present up to eighteen months or so, depending on the situation.

You can start with smaller lifestyle issues then move to the larger ones, such as church attendance and beliefs. Perhaps your children will want to offer their own ideas about what is important to them. These can be worked into your Freedom Plan. You can even put it all in writing and jointly sign the agreement.

As radical as this may seem, it is probably the only way to go from a very restrictive family environment to a more open one. No one can guarantee you success at this point, but I am confident your children's response will be positive. What is more, your prospects for working through these problems will be promising.

But, you ask, what if you grant your teenagers this freedom and it turns out wrong? What if your kids happily accept their new liberty and go out and do that which grieves you?

If you have made it clear that to do so will bring definitive consequences, I say grant freedom anyway. Your children may well be doing these things already without your knowledge. Your freedom granting, if it does nothing else, will bring the problems out into the open. If they persist in their rebellion and activities that you have named as unacceptable, you will have little choice but to carry through with the consequences you have also named. An organization called "Tough Love," which has local chapters in most areas of the country, can provide specialized help for parents with particularly difficult teenagers.

In all of this, the bottom line remains that freedom is a critical issue when it comes to an authentic faith for your teenagers. This approach to teenage rebellion has respected support from Dr. Roy Zuck and Dr. Gene Getz, professors at Dallas Theological Seminary, one of America's leading evangelical seminaries. In their book, *Christian Youth: An In-Depth Study*, Dr. Zuck and Dr. Getz conclude that even when teenagers appear to be rejecting the faith and values of their parents, at heart they are still clinging to the religious faith of their parents and home. Given a real choice at this critical period in their lives, Zuck and Getz believe that Christian young people more often than not will choose to follow the faith of their homes and churches.[6]

Leading Your Children to an Authentic Faith

In closing this chapter about freedom, I want to briefly summarize these points and add a thought or two.

1. *Aim for authenticity.* Tell your children you want them to be real people personally, emotionally and spiritually. Teach and model the faith you believe and the lifestyle you endorse. Then, at the right times and in the right proportions, let your children choose to accept or reject those beliefs and that lifestyle.

Teach, promote, declare and invite, but do not force your faith on your children. Instead, wisely encourage them to choose. A chosen faith is internal and real; an imposed faith is external and superficial. The latter may please parents and friends for a while, but in the end it often leads to heartaches for all.

2. *Decide to let go.* Above all, decide to be a freedom-granting parent. Whether your children are very young and ready for only the most basic freedoms or whether they are teenagers engaged in a daily war of independence with you, they need the freedom only you can give them. You have parent power. Deliberately plan to give your children the freedom to choose. Play no games, either verbal or emotional. Be a freedom giver and defuse the need for teenage rebellion before it becomes an issue.

3. *With freedom require responsibility.* Letting go is not casting adrift. As you give your children freedom you must require them to be accountable to you until they are fully adult and fully free. You must also teach them that they are accountable to themselves and to God. Teach your children that their choices have consequences for themselves and for others. Be fair but firm, because freedom without responsibility and accountability is as dangerous to your children as no freedom.

4. *Make room for failure.* Every Christian parent longs to see their children grow up to be mature Christians who make wise decisions. All our prayers and efforts aim themselves to that end. We long to see our children grow in Christ to be mature, strong, winsome believers. But sometimes things go wrong. Life doesn't always turn out the way we plan. Despite our best efforts, our children can make wrong choices. When they do, we will do well not to rush in and fix things up. Sometimes all that is left for parents is a prayerful, trusting silence. Part of learning how to make right choices is making wrong ones.

5. *Remember the Shepherd.* He gave His life for His sheep. We know that He searches for wandering, lost sheep even when others have given up. We can rest in His love for us and them. He will be faithful to us and them to the very end.

If you had a hundred sheep and *one* of them strayed away and was lost in the wilderness, wouldn't you leave the ninety-nine others to go and search for the lost one until you found it? And then you would joyfully carry it home on your shoulders. When you arrived you would call together your friends and neighbors to rejoice with you because your lost sheep was found.

Well, in the same way heaven will be happier over the one lost sinner who returns to God than over ninety-nine others who haven't strayed away! (Luke 15:4-7, TLB)

Recommended Reading

The Grace Awakening by Charles R. Swindoll (Word Publishing, Dallas, 1990).

Traveling Light: Reflections on the Free Life by Eugene H. Peterson (InterVarsity Press, Downers Grove, IL, 1982).

10

"X" Factors in Faith Rejection

Everyone knows that life is neither tidy nor predictable. Just when we think we've got it all together, when the problems seem solved and the worst dangers are past, unexpected things happen that can profoundly change our lives.

Sometimes these "X" factors directly affect our families and our efforts to pass our faith on to our children. Events over which we have little control can create major problems. When the dust settles, we are left without answers, unable to do little more than pray and cast ourselves upon the Lord. Let me illustrate by telling you about Karen.

Karen was born into a Christian family. She grew up in a faith-filled atmosphere in which she went to church and saw the Christian life lived in her home. When she was young, she made a confession of faith and gave evidence of being a Christian. Her father was a successful salesman and her mother was a teacher.

They were bright, educated, dedicated Christian people who loved their children and had a better-than-average relationship with them.

At first, things went pretty well in Karen's life, spiritually speaking. She went to church readily, was involved in Sunday school and youth ministries, and generally seemed headed in the right direction, including attending a Christian college. It all looked right, but there was an "X" factor in the mix which no one ever thought about—except Karen, who no doubt felt the pressure of this variable long before it ever made its ominous presence fully known to others.

Karen was physically unattractive. A tall, slender girl without the requisite American figure, she was also homely looking and quiet in personality. When it came to boys, Karen wasn't in the running. In fact, she wasn't even on the list. All through her teenage and young adult years, her friends were girls like herself—outsiders looking in, wishing, hoping, longing.

It worked for a while. Her mother and father were understanding and helpful in the ways they were able. But by the time Karen finished college, she was a lonely, frustrated young woman. She knew the biblical standards for male/female relationships: purity and propriety. She also knew the Christian rules: Don't chase and don't compromise. Church was the place where rules were applied with the most force, a fact which compounded the issue.

By the time she was twenty-five, Karen knew she had a decision to make. She could embrace a faithful Christian life filled with social loneliness and sexual frustration, or she could turn from the straight and narrow and seek comfort and companionship in the same way she knew many of her girl friends at work did— through impropriety and impurity. However unattractive she was, she knew what most men wanted from a woman. And she was fairly certain they would accept it from her no matter what she looked like. She also knew that if she were willing to go along on this point, she might even be able to snag a guy like herself, who had his own problems in meeting girls.

Karen chose to seek out male companionship no matter what it might cost her. She was well aware that other women in her situation had chosen the way of the cross and a single life despite the resulting loneliness and frustration. She knew the single missionary stories. But she would not take that route. Her path would be along the way of social activities, singles bars, dances and any other means by which she could meet guys. Any guys. And she met them. Today Karen is living with a man she bumped into one night in a smoke-filled, booze-drenched joint. He's getting what he wants and she's getting what she wants.

Obviously, Karen isn't going to church on Sunday mornings these days. Or any other times. Her parents are stunned and hurt. They had done it all "right" so far as good parenting was concerned. They played with their kids, prayed with their kids and did what they thought they should as good Christian parents. Never once did they imagine that something as basic as their daughter's physical appearance, a reality of life over which neither they nor she had any control, would eventually play a major role in her unwillingness to follow the Lord.

And so it is that the "X" factor of physical unattractiveness produced a painful social isolation and profound frustration that came to be hated and feared by a young Christian woman. I'm sure at one time Karen wanted to do what was right, to serve the Lord and follow Him in all her ways. Had you interviewed her at age sixteen, I think you would have found very little evidence of the deadly spiritual disease to which she finally succumbed.

Secular research backs up Karen's experience: Never-married people have the highest rates of defection from the Christian faith. Singleness by itself, these researchers report, creates the environment most likely to adversely affect the values of the faith in which these singles grew up.[1] Let's hear it for more and better singles ministries! Other lonely, hurting Karens are out there. Let's reach out to them so they can be strengthened and encouraged in their faith as they confront the real problems of life.

Yet however much empathy and understanding Karen deserves, her choice cannot be justified. She knew better (and surely still does) but went against her principles and the doctrines of her Christian faith. Make no mistake. It was a tough choice. Anyone who hasn't been there should not cast stones.

Does Karen's plight, seen from this vantage point, lessen her parents' pain? Does the realization that their daughter faced special pressures and problems they did not fully appreciate give them any comfort today? Probably not. They must live with the results of an unpredictable variable that intruded into their family: physical unattractiveness.

Would attractiveness have changed Karen's situation enough that this problem might not have occurred? If the constant social isolation she endured had not existed, would she have been less vulnerable to Satan's devices in her life? It would seem so. But no one can be certain. Had she been pretty she might have made the same choice but for a different reason. In the end, it all came down to a personal choice on Karen's part, no matter what her circumstances dictated. She made her own decision to go her own way.

Other "X" Factors

The "X" factor in faith rejection can show up in other ways. Personal tragedies can turn people away from God. A shocking, unexpected abandonment by a spouse can create emotional and psychological damage with related ripple effects that eventually push people away from their faith. Need we say anything about the effects of child abuse on the prospects of a healthy Christian faith? Divorce can be an "X" factor in faith rejection for both spouses as well as their children. One study revealed a significant correlation between the unhappiness and family trauma caused by divorce and a high incidence of faith dropout.[2]

Dysfunctional family or church life can also introduce "X" factors into the process of faith formation. In these situations, the gospel gets mixed up with tormented human relationships or misapplied and over-applied doctrines so that it becomes difficult for people, especially teens and young adults, to separate what is right and good about the gospel from what troubles them at home and church.

Garrison Keillor, the radio personality known for his Lake Wobegon stories, grew up in a Bible-believing church. In an interview with *Leadership* magazine, Keillor names his church's focus on "the principle of separation" as one of the reasons he walked away from his childhood faith. For Keillor, this separation principle became the "very sort of legalism that Christ was continuously rebuking in the Pharisees who were following Him around."[3]

Then Keillor makes this observation: "My church seemed to find ample reason to separate themselves from almost everybody, even to separate themselves from each other. That track, if followed to its natural conclusion, would lead to churches made up of individuals breaking bread alone in their living rooms across America."[4]

Thus a particular view of the Christian life practiced to the extreme became an "X" factor in the faith choices of a gifted young man growing up in the church. Did anyone know how the little boy felt or what he was thinking? The article suggests indirectly that Keillor's parents agreed with their church's practice of fierce separation from the world. It was his unpredictable reaction to it that resulted in his choice to leave the faith of his home and family. Possibly his parents never understood his decision to "walk away" from his childhood faith, but surely they were pained by his struggle and his ultimate choice. Keillor attends church today but not one in the Bible church tradition of his family.

Homosexuality is yet another "X" factor. This is not the place to examine the question of the origins of homosexuality.[5] But it is the place to make the point that the torment and alienation that are an inescapable part of this problem profoundly affect one's faith choices. The Bible says homosexual practice is sin. Can anyone miss the choices that homosexual young men or women must make in these circumstances? And who will help them if the church doesn't?

For a number of years I have served on the board of Regeneration, a local ministry organized to help people who are seeking a way out of homosexuality. Sometimes those who come for help are people who grew up in evangelical Christian homes and churches. When I hear their pain-filled stories I realize how negatively their faith was affected by their profound problems with their sexual identity. Little did their parents suspect the evil nature or power of the foe they were fighting as they tried to teach their children the way of Christ.

Even after these courageous souls choose to receive Christ and break with their homosexual past, their journey to emotional and spiritual wholeness is fraught with dangers and difficulties. Their testimonies of deliverance and healing, as well as their determination to live intensely disciplined lives, make me ponder my own testimony and Christian lifestyle. At the same time, I know that these joyful stories of victory represent only a small part of the large and difficult problem of homosexuality. I know, too, that homosexuality is one of life's unexpected troubles that adversely affects faith choices in every life it touches.

Your Child's Personality as an "X" Factor

Sometimes personality itself can be an "X" factor. Some kids are going to do what they want to do no matter what. In the next chapter I discuss the role of personality in spirituality, which is essentially a discussion about two basic personality types: pro-authority and anti-authority (or compliant and non-compliant). That is not what I am talking about here. I am talking about those unpredictable, uncontrollable kids who have arrived by birth in Christian homes from time immemorial.

My wife and I are blessed with two compliant children. No wonder it all seems so easy! But I have talked with enough hurting parents who have had a sprinkling of both compliant and non-compliant children ... and one (or more) who was off the charts. No matter what approach these parents took—whether kindness, understanding or choice, or toughness, discipline and take-no-prisoners—these special kinds of kids would not listen, would not cooperate, would not do what their parents asked or directed them to do.

Sometimes their behavior was loud, violent and rebellious. In other cases, their response to parental direction was quiet, non-violent but still rebellious. Nothing worked. As soon as these kids could leave their home and their faith, they left—even while their brothers and sisters stayed. Same family, same environment, same genes, different behavior. Sad, troubling, inexplicable facts.

Did I hear someone say, "You have to get to these kinds of kids when they're toddlers"? I agree wholeheartedly. Get to them literally before they can stand on their own feet. Show them love and show them who's in charge. Teach them about God and teach them about life. And make sure you start praying at the same time.

Sometimes getting to these kind of kids early is still too late. I have seen two- and three-year-olds who were as stubborn and rebellious at that age as they were at twelve or thirteen. They could be threatened, spanked and punished for their behavior and it made little or no difference. They couldn't be frightened, loved, cajoled or rewarded into changing their ways and attitudes. They seemed almost to come from another race of human beings.

Not long ago I was watching a sports event on television. At halftime I began to flip through the channels, looking for something more interesting than most halftimes have to offer. I came upon a family fight much like the ones I have been describing. I was hooked into the story immediately. The teenage son was accusing the parents of not understanding him; the parents were accusing the son of being a troublemaker who wouldn't listen to them.

As I watched the story unfold, I found myself being whipsawed back and forth between child and parents. At times, both sides seemed equally right. The context was so correct, the problems so realistic and the dialogue so true to life, I couldn't turn away. At times the filmmaker cleverly pulled the viewer into the decision-making process, thus allowing me to make right or wrong decisions in this drama of family life gone awry.

The sports event never had a chance. *Tough Love,* which was the title of the film (it can be rented for VCR use), easily won. I'm certain its setting and dialogue had come from many real-life experiences. I watched the story unfold to its conclusion. The ending was positive, if not Alice-in-Wonderland. The viewer came away with hope, and with a heavy dose of realism about how some kids do what they want no matter what their parents try. I especially recall one line where the father, bewildered and no longer the strong, self-confident dad, says to a Tough Love group: "I can't understand it. Being kind and sensitive worked with Scott" (his other son).

Some kids come into the world with stubborn, uncontrollable personalities. No doubt tough love works with some of them. But I'm certain a film could be made where the story doesn't end quite so well as the one I watched. In this kind of movie, tough love would mean that the parents must learn to accept the outcome, whatever it is, and to do that without self-blame.

Fortunately, the "X" factors which affect faith rejection are not the dominant reasons why most people who grow up in Christian homes leave the faith. But it does happen and it is worth knowing. When you do your best, when you're aware, sensitive and loving, when you practice all the rules of tough love, and it still comes out wrong because an unpredictable factor pushed its way into your lives, all you can do is trust God and pray. Take your burden to the Lord and leave it there. He cares for your son or daughter at least as much as you do, "X" factor and all.

11

Does Personality Affect Spirituality?

One of my favorite family pictures is of our son Jon at the age of six or seven months. To snap this photographic gem, I placed Jon on his back in his playpen. Then I reached for my camera and shot a picture straight down as he looked up at me.

In this picture Jon is smiling slightly in response to a little cooing on my part. His arms are at his side. He doesn't move as I focus. He looks just like all the happy, contented babies you see in magazines and television ads promoting comfortable diapers or the right baby food.

It wasn't a fluke. I could have put little Jon in that

playpen any day of the month and he would have responded in the same way. From the moment he came into this world, he was quiet, easygoing and cooperative.

The same cannot be said for our daughter Tina. When I put her in the same playpen at age seven months, she would roll over immediately, get up on her hands and knees and crawl to the edge of the playpen. Then she would try to stand by taking hold of the netting and pulling herself up. From the moment she came into this world, she was active, feisty and strong-willed.

Conclusion? Jon and Tina are different. And both have retained their distinctive personality traits to this day. While both are basically cooperative, they still remain different despite being born of the same parents, growing up in the same home and receiving the same love and care.

Psychiatrist Ross Campbell believes that all children can be placed in one of two basic personality types: pro-authority and anti-authority. In Dr. Campbell's view, three-fourths of all children are anti-authority in their personality makeup. These are the kids who come into the world wanting to move your rules aside. The other one-fourth are pro-authority. Their basic approach to life is, "What can I do to help you, Mom and Dad?"[1]

According to Dr. Campbell, neither personality is bad. That's the good news, although I'm sure a lot of parents would be hard-pressed to describe as "good news" an unmanageable, anti-authority child, not to mention two or three in one family!

What Dr. Campbell means is that personality in and of itself does not make a child good or bad. Personality is simply a beginning point, a combination of genetic traits from which a person develops a pattern of behaviors and emotions.[2]

The important point is that parents *understand* their children's personalities. This is especially true when it comes to passing our faith on to them.

Clearly, an anti-authority child needs a different approach than a pro-authority child. Trying to push the Christian faith down the throat of an unwilling, anti-authority child is a sure prescription for faith rejection. Why? Because these kids arrive on your doorstep with the inborn trait of wanting to think and decide for themselves. Forcing them violates their most basic personality characteristic and virtually guarantees a negative reaction either at the moment of conflict or in a later "get even" situation.[3]

When confronted by an anti-authoritarian child, parents often react by becoming rigid, severe disciplinarians. They insist on their children doing exactly as they say—my way or the highway. Parents then seek to reinforce their position by taking their children to a church where the same rules apply.

Far from solving the problem of a rebellious, anti-authority child, this overly authoritarian approach creates an angry reaction which results in intense clashes in the home. And it can lead to faith rejection as well. In Dr. Campbell's opinion, the intensely authoritarian and rigidly disciplinarian approach, both at home and in church, is the principle reason so many anti-authoritarian kids "turn against the church."[4]

As you know from what I have said in this book, I believe the reasons for faith rejection are more complicated than simply being too authoritarian with your children, no matter what their personality type. But I have no doubt that misunderstanding an anti-authority personality in a child can be a significant factor in faith rejection.

Raising the Anti-Authoritarian Child

Well and good you say, but what now? If an overly authoritarian, rigidly disciplinarian approach is not the way to deal with anti-authority children, what angle should a parent take? Let them do what they want? Neglect them?

Not for a moment.

Dr. Campbell recommends what he calls the *authoritative* approach. This is based on direction and correction that flow out of unconditional love. No matter who children are or what they do, they are worthy of being loved by their parents. But this does not mean Mom and Dad must therefore accept or ignore the wrongful or sinful actions and attitudes of their children. Unconditional love is not the same as "hands off" parenting.

Years ago, preachers often took a "love the sinner, hate the sin" view of the gospel, a concept that has its roots in God's love for sinful humanity. But God's unconditional love also requires that God's holiness be satisfied. Sinners cannot get off scot-free. God's righteousness and justice require more: the atoning death of Christ for sin and judgment upon sinners who reject His salvation.

Similarly, direction and correction must be applied to children who know what is right but refuse to do it. Unconditional parental love, which belongs to every child by birthright, must also be tough. Authoritative parents will understand and correct their child's misbehavior and disobedience. Strong, sturdy discipline, including withdrawal of privileges and appropriate corporal punishment, where age and circumstance allow, will follow.

In *Kids Who Follow, Kids Who Don't*, Dr. Campbell cites a case study in which four types of parenting were studied: authoritarian, permissive, neglecting and authoritative. This study revealed that children reared under the authoritative method not only identified with their parents' values, but made it safely through the dangerous anti-authority years and embraced the religious beliefs their parents were trying to pass on to them.

On the other hand, people who grew up in strongly authoritarian homes showed up with the highest percentage of faith rejection in the study. They were also the most emotionally unsettled individuals in the four groups of people surveyed. The results of the study, says Dr. Campbell, demonstrate that "children who are lovingly disciplined and guided to adulthood, will eventually not only adopt, but *want* to adopt their parents' spiritual values."[5]

Raising a Pro-Authority Child

What about the 25 percent who come into the world with pro-authority personalities?

These are the kids who are easy to manage. They're neat, fun youngsters who are eager to please their parents and just about anyone else in a position of authority. They do this because their personality type needs approval and acceptance. But this willingness to go along with their parents can create major problems as these pro-authority children get older.

Imagine for a moment a well-disciplined son or daughter one day suddenly exploding in a fit of anger. Picture a does-all-the-right-things teenager or young adult becoming depressed and withdrawn. Reflect on the possibility of an active-in-the-youth-group young man dropping out of church and all the Christian activities that were so much a part of his life. Imagine trying to correct your usually cooperative daughter one day and hearing her tell you to get off her back, or worse, to get out of her life.

These are not nightmare scenarios. They happen in real life. Why? Because parents of pro-authority daughters or sons tend to take advantage of them by expecting and, yes, even by demanding that these pleasant, "How can I help you, Mom and Dad?" kids do what they are told and believe everything they hear.

Unaware that they are taking advantage of their child's willingness to cooperate, parents often get what they want from these children by using the nastiest parental control-and-manipulation tool of all: guilt. All they have to do is express disappointment at wrong actions or attitudes, or hint at (or threaten) non-acceptance because their son or daughter said the wrong thing, and the pro-authority child backs off and does whatever the parent wants. It seems like easy parenting.

But a day of reckoning is coming. While these pro-authority kids may be cooperative and pleasant, they also need to make their own choices about their faith. They need to be respected and given as much room and sensitivity as their anti-authority siblings. If they are denied the right to make important faith decisions, they will have a faith that does not belong to them. They will also have an underlying anger that can erupt at any time against their home and the Christian faith.

Not only must parents understand this facet of their pro-authority children, but they must also intentionally help their kids begin making their own faith-and-life decisions. Pro-authority children by nature are willing to let others choose for them. That makes it easy for parents in the short run, but dangerous for the long run, especially if parents don't back off and let these kids start making their own choices in life.

When our son Jon was fourteen, he announced that he no longer wished to go to church. Despite his easygoing personality, I knew that underneath this young man's cooperative exterior lay a stubbornness and streak of independence that could be traced to, of all people, his father. I also knew that he needed to make these kinds of decisions himself. Still, his announcement surprised me. It was his first significant "I'm taking over my life" announcement, and it sounded strange and was a little unnerving. In any case, his mother and I decided it was time for our freedom doctrine to kick in. We told him as calmly as we could (though we weren't nearly so steady behind our cool masks) that if he did not wish to go to church anymore, that was okay by us. We would go without him. He had come to the place in his life where it was time for him to make those kinds of decisions for himself.

Jon stayed home for two weeks. During this time he attended the Church of the Inner Spring. Then without a word he got up on the third Sunday morning, got ready for church and went with us. Except for sickness, I don't think he has missed a Sunday since. In fact, he has become actively involved with the young people in his church fellowship and works part-time for the church.

I have sometimes wondered what we would have done if Jon had never gone back to church. I know some parents that has happened to. In fact, I know some parents whose children announced that they would no longer attend church and never did again, at least to this point. I even know one young woman who not only refuses to attend church, but who mocks her pastor father's ministry publicly as well. Talk about parents in pain! How very much I admire those people, especially those in ministry, who carry on despite the heartbreak of children who are away from God.

Please understand that I am not trying to portray our home as an especially understanding or wise place when it comes to parenting. I know that our children's strong faith is only partly the result of our sensitivity to their personalities or any other wisdom we may have applied in Christian child rearing. I assure you that as parents we messed up more times than I am prepared to confess. I also know that we had two pretty good, easy-to-rear kids.

The truth is that my wife and I owe a debt to all the people who were part of our children's spiritual growth and maturity, from their grandparents and Christian camp in the summer to Christian teachers in public schools and youth groups at church. All are part of the package that God used to produce these wonderful, strong-in-the-faith young adults. That fact is pretty much true in every case where kids turn out well.

Training Up a Child . . .

My point in this chapter is simply to encourage you to understand your kids. Their personalities are part of their faith experience. To know them well and deal with them accordingly is to lead them to salvation and to help them live joyfully and fully for Christ. Surely it is natural and right that the God who made us would also make it possible for us to know ourselves and our children so this could happen.[6]

Perhaps the most famous statement in the Bible relating to child rearing is Proverbs 22:6 which instructs parents to "train up a child in the way he should go, and when he is old he will not depart from it." Several views exist regarding the meaning of this verse. According to some commentators, the real meaning of this verse is parental understanding of the child.

According to this view, Proverbs 22:6 is not a blanket promise or law that children who are taught sound Christian doctrine will grow up to be faithful followers of Christ. Instead, it is a proverb, a snippet of wisdom about child rearing with the emphasis on the word *should* rather than the words *will not.*

The distinction is critical. If we know our children well, we will train them in the way they *should* be taught, that is, according to their dispositions.[7] If we train them in a way they should *not* be taught, that is, in a manner or style that gives little or no thought to their personalities, we prompt their resistance to us and our faith.

Parents naturally do what seems right to them. This usually means rearing our kids the way we ourselves were reared. In some situations it's the best a mother and father can do. Still, we need to believe that it is possible to wisely and confidently "train up" our children so that they *will not* depart from that faith. If we ignore our children's inborn dispositions and press them into Christian cookie cutter molds, we flout the creator God who intentionally made each of us individuals.

Think about it. A God who made it a point to design every fingerprint differently, not to mention every face, every body and every genetic code, surely must have taken special care to give each of us our own unique personalities. When we work with our children in this light, we honor the God who created us and them.

Train your children in the way of Jesus Christ. Teach them. Discipline them. Make them disciples. But be careful to do it according to their dispositions. Pay attention to their God-given personalities. Then confidently claim the promise of Proverbs 22:6 that your children will not depart from this way even when they are old.

Opinion Legislation

by Brennan Bagwell and Scott Elkins

She's always been a good girl,
    tried to please her mom and dad.
She practices her music
    and does the best she can.

The preacher lays the law down,
    better listen to the man.
Just worry about obeyin'
    you don't have to understand.

We've gotta give a reason,
    in a way they understand,
Not opinion legislation that
    drives our good kids bad.

The pressures and the changes
    seem to multiply with time.
But the rules that she's obeyin'
    were never realigned.

CHORUS: Oh, but where's the love they're
    needing?
Where is the love they're
    seeking?
They need our arms around them,
    not the chains that only weaken.

She's standing on the edge now,
    her pretty face so sad.
We really shouldn't wonder
    why our good kids turn out bad.

She's standing on the edge now
    looking at the world

Be careful how you push her.
You may lose your little girl.

• • • • • • • • • • • • • • • • • • •

12

Perfect Christian Kids

Peer pressure is a relatively new term in the English language. You can't find it in the *Oxford English Dictionary*. Even the less formal, slang-accepting *Roget's Thesaurus* omits it. But every Christian parent knows what it is.

Peer pressure is the vague but very real pull or push people feel from their friends and associates to conform to the standard around them. It's the pressure to earn as much, live as well, dress the same, think similarly. Sometimes it can be positive, such as the pressure older Christian kids can exert on younger kids to play it straight. But mostly, peer pressure is negative.

Christian parents are especially concerned about the peer pressure their children feel at school and in their other group associations. They know their kids are faced daily with intimidation by others who want them to conform to the prevailing teen views and attitudes about life.

Peer pressure. It's nasty business.

Would you believe that today's Christian parents are feeling a peer pressure all their own? It is as real and unrelenting as anything teenagers feel. And it produces just as much anxiety and fear.

What is this parental peer pressure? It's Perfect Christian Kids. It's the unarticulated but widely accepted belief that unless you rear emotionally healthy, spiritually zealous, impervious-to-culture kids, you have failed (or come close) as a Christian parent.

The origins of this new parental peer pressure can be traced to the good parenting/strong families movement of the last twenty years. This praiseworthy Christian movement, which was a reaction to the social and moral upheaval of the '60s and '70s, set its sights on rebuilding and strengthening Christian families in America.

It's safe to say that the good parenting/strong families movement has succeeded. It has provided parents with guidance, support and encouragement amid the enormous challenges of rearing children in a society stacked against Christian families. It has increased the parenting sensitivities of moms and dads everywhere and has succeeded in creating a national awareness of the importance of the family in American society. When has the United States government ever been so concerned about child-related issues as it is today?

But out of these achievements, which I applaud heartily, has emerged the troubling idea that the highest goal to which modern Christian parents can aspire is the spiritual well-being of their children. Profoundly (and rightfully) disturbed by the dangers of a pervasively evil culture, Christian parents are readily sacrificing everything for their children, including spousal relationships and their own emotional and spiritual well-being.

This mistaken view of parenting promises trouble for all concerned, something I will explore a little later in this chapter. First, allow me to tell you the true story of Harry and Phil. Their father held them in such high esteem it virtually set them up for spiritual disaster and it caused him to fail in his ministry.

What Can Happen When Priorities Get Confused

Harry and Phil were two brothers who walked away from their faith big time. Not willing to simply reject the faith of their home and church, they mocked that faith and their parents by living immoral, dishonest lives.

What makes Harry and Phil's story especially compelling is that they were preacher's kids. Nothing makes the church grapevine like a couple of PKs gone bad. Everyone who knew the family knew the boys. And everyone, it seemed, wanted the father to straighten out his sons before they made an even bigger mess of their lives and the church, which eventually they did.

I know about PKs because I am one. It's a club to which you must belong before you can appreciate the special dangers and pressures that come with membership. Interested? Being a preacher's kid means that neighbors and church members expect you to be a good little boy all the time. It means your Sunday school teachers expect you to know the answers to all their questions. And it means that your friends at school and in the neighborhood are amazed (to your face) that you don't go to the movies, play cards or go to dances. It means you're different.

Actually, preacher's kids are just like everyone else with one exception: They have to play with the deacon's kids. That's the *real* reason PKs get into so much trouble. Just kidding, of course. But make no mistake. Preacher's kids face a tougher-than-usual challenge in life. When they take a hike, they can usually tell you why.

All of which brings me back to Harry and Phil and a confession that I must make: Harry and Phil are pseudonyms. In this case, I did not use their real names because I wanted their story, which is true in every detail, to sound more real, more end-of-the-twentieth century and thus more applicable to your life and mine.

Actually, Harry and Phil are the two sons of Eli, who was a high priest and judge of Israel before that nation became a monarchy. Harry and Phil are Hophni and Phineas—two preacher's kids who took the all-time walk away from the faith in which they grew up.

Hophni and Phineas were so spiritually corrupt, so morally reprehensible, that we still use a word associated with them to describe the worst possible spiritual condition of a church or ministry: Ichabod, meaning, "The glory of the Lord has departed." You can read about it in 1 Samuel 2:12—4:22.

Perhaps Eli is best known because of the story of the boy Samuel and his unusual call by God to serve in the temple. That is an inspiring account to be sure. But the really important point about Eli is the trouble in his home and the spiritual havoc that resulted because of the wickedness of his sons.

Temple priests by birthright, these preacher's kids failed every test of spiritual integrity. "The sons of Eli were scoundrels," 1 Samuel 2:12 records, "who cared nothing for Jehovah" (JB). They abused their religious authority, lived in open immorality and wilfully scandalized their father. Scoundrel preachers!

This troubling story would be easier to accept if Eli himself had been a spiritual failure. One could then say that his boys did little more than follow in the footsteps of their father. But the fact is, Eli was a godly man full of zeal for the Lord and the temple. Surely his sons saw these wonderful qualities in their father, yet they chose another path.

Why? What happened? How could two boys from a home like this go so wrong? How could two boys grow up in an environment as spiritually intense as this and not "know the Lord" as we are told at the outset of the story? (1 Samuel 2:12) In the Demas story we had to do a little guessing. In this story we know exactly what happened because the Bible tells us.

We know, for example, that Eli was preoccupied at the temple. It may have been otherwise, but so far as the record is concerned, Eli had very little fatherly involvement with his boys. He seems utterly absorbed in doing God's work while his sons do whatever they want.

In today's jargon we would call Eli a workaholic. He was great in the pulpit and performed his ministerial duties energetically and effectively. But he was not as good at home or on the playground. Faithful in serving God, he was less than faithful about spending time with his boys.

We also know that Eli did not discipline his sons. Even when he was home, he apparently made no effort to correct Hophni and Phineas. He was a softie. The boy's mother couldn't even threaten to "tell dad when he gets home" because even if she did, he wouldn't do anything about their disobedience, disrespect and dishonesty. If we were grading him, we would have to give Eli straight fs in the department of discipline.

Eli could not plead ignorance. People told him about Hophni and Phineas. The Bible says he "was aware of what was going on around him. He knew, for instance, that his sons were seducing the young women who assisted at the entrance of the Tabernacle" (1 Samuel 2:22, TLB).

He also knew that his sons did not care what he or others thought. When he finally tried to restrain Hophni and Phineas, Eli spoke pleadingly rather than authoritatively to them. "Why do you do such things? For I hear of your evil dealings from all the people" (1 Samuel 2:23, NKJV). Their response was to shrug him off. Why should they do anything else, especially now that he was an old man? It was a case of too little, too late.

Eli's lack of discipline was related to another problem in his relationship with his sons. This time the trouble was all of his making: He loved them too much. We know this because the Bible says he "honored" his sons more than God (1 Samuel 2:29, TLB). It was a confusion of priorities one does not expect from a spiritually mature man.

Eli's mega-fondness for his boys was the fatal flaw in his fathering. His willingness to put Hophni and Phineas on a pedestal above God, which was a kind of idolatry, distorted his vision of God and undermined his high calling as a priest of Israel and a father to his children. And we must not forget, it brought the judgment of God upon him and his family.

There is a postscript to the Hophni and Phineas story. It's the Joel and Abijah story. Remember them? Unfair question.

Joel and Abijah were the sons of Samuel, Eli's protégé and heir apparent. They grew up, in and around the temple and watched Hophni and Phineas in action. Twenty or so years younger than Eli's sons, they missed nothing. In fact, it all seemed normal to them because they grew up in a home that was much like Eli's.

Think about it. Samuel learned his fathering by watching Eli. Eli's preoccupation with temple work, the lack of discipline and his inordinate affection for his sons were Samuel's model of how a home operates. Apparently he bought it, lock, stock and barrel.

The outcome was the same. Joel and Abijah rejected their father's faith just as Hophni and Phineas rejected Eli's faith. And just as God took away Eli's priestly line through the untimely death of his sons, so the elders of Israel rejected Joel and Abijah because of their wickedness.

It was at this point in Israel's history that the leaders of the nation asked God for a new kind of rule: monarchy. "Now make us a king to judge us like all the nations," they demanded (1 Samuel 8:5, NKJV). Even though they had good reason for asking for a change of leadership, they were nonetheless rejecting God's rule through priests and judges. Their decision was the beginning of Israel's spiritual decline.

Talk about the long reach of parenting! Samuel's family problems which were linked to Eli's family problems were the first steps down the slippery slope that eventually took the people away from God and brought them at last to the place of judgment and disintegration as a nation. Had Eli known what his fatherly over-love would bring Israel, it might have prompted him to take decisive action. But he did not.

A Mistake in Modern Parenting

Christian parents today will probably have a hard time relating to Eli. Our good parenting mindset is miles away from him. His failure to discipline his flagrantly wicked sons, who were under his spiritual authority even as adults, was so wrong and so weak we cannot identify with him.

Yet there is a sense in which Eli was a very modern parent. His over-love for his sons, which was the fundamental issue so far as God was concerned, was not all that far removed from the position in which Christian parents find themselves today. Our readiness to put our children first in our lives is in some ways a present-day version of Eli's mistake.

The Scriptures definitively establish that other aspects of the Christian life precede our children in God's scheme of things. The apostle Paul's instructions to believers in Ephesians 5 and 6, which set the standard for the Body of Christ in all ages, make it crystal clear that believers have a priority of spiritual responsibilities to which they are called: the worship of God, conformity to the image of Christ, maturity of Christian character, faithfulness in life and witness, and *finally* family life and bringing up children in the "training and admonition of the Lord" (Ephesians 6:4).

Children are not at the apex of the Christian value system. We love them intensely and we want the best for them personally and spiritually. But when we place them first, however honorable our motives, we dishonor God and create problems for ourselves and for them.

So then, what is the point? Stop loving your kids? Let go of your parental responsibilities? Of course not.

The point is, stop making Perfect Christian Kids the ultimate goal of Christian parenting. Stop trying to produce perfect little saints. It can't be done nor does God expect that it should. Christian maturity involves struggle and growth. Our children are going to have moments when it seems they haven't learned a thing we've tried so hard to teach them. At times they are going to be difficult, disobedient and disgusting. That's part of the growing-up process. To expect perfection is to stir up needless fear and guilt in parents and unnecessary anxiety and resistance in children.

One Final Question

I conclude this chapter by raising a question. Is it possible that over-loving our children is a subconscious attempt to ensure that they will love us in return? Is the desire for Perfect Christian Kids, as lofty and pure as that goal seems, actually a misplaced spiritual priority by which we hunger for our children's love instead of hungering for God's love? To be loved by your children is one of life's greatest joys. What parent does not long for it? But to accept this as a substitute for loving God and being loved by Him is to settle for the good rather than the best.

Oswald Chambers, one of the twentieth century's great devotional writers, says that "love means deliberate self-limitation." In this quote Chambers means that Christians must intentionally limit their own interests so they can fully identify themselves with the "interests of our Lord in everything."[1]

This kind of love means deliberately limiting ourselves as parents so our children can be free to love us and the Savior. It means limiting ourselves so we do not esteem or honor them above God. It means not over-loving them and not over-involving ourselves in their lives, protecting, guiding, fixing and deciding for them until they are smothered to death.

Mom and Dad, love your children with all your hearts. It's their birthright. They don't have to do anything to earn it. Let them live in the confidence that no matter what happens, you will always love them even though you may have to reject what they do.

But don't over-love them. Don't pressure them to be Perfect Christian Kids. If you do, you'll put them in the same bind as the perfect parenting bind you've put upon yourself. Perfect Christian Kids are not possible. Let your love be disciplined, yet total and free. Give your children this bedrock for their lives and one day they will rise up and call you blessed.

13

A Reason for Hope

In a book like this, it's easy to get focused on negatives. Losing faith, dropping out and leaving are not exactly the stuff of exhilaration and hope. But these realities come with the territory. You can't talk about why people who grew up in Christian homes leave the faith unless you look at why people who grew up in Christian homes *leave* the faith.

Yet amid the discouragement, there is hope and joy. Why? Because sooner or later, so many of the people who leave the faith come back. While a great deal of statistical data is not available on this subject, what does exist shows conclusively that most dropouts are temporary leavers.

In one extensive survey, Dr. James Dobson found that 85 percent of even the most severely rebellious dropouts returned to their parents' basic religious faith and values by the time they were twenty-four years old. Dobson also suggests that the rate of return probably would be even higher if his survey had included people up to the age of thirty-five. His study shows that dropouts tend to return to the religious beliefs and values of their homes as they get older.[1]

No one knows how many people actually leave the Christian faith. That figure could only be obtained by surveying everyone born and reared in a Christian home or converted to the Christian faith at some time during their life. Obviously that kind of information cannot be obtained unless Uncle Sam wants to include a question about it when taking the national census. Even then the denominational and doctrinal distinctions necessary to get at the information needed would make such a survey virtually impossible. The point to remember is simply that the 85 percent return rate applies to *known* faith dropouts.

Research on faith rejection also indicates that a high rate of return among known leavers holds true among churches and religious groups of all kinds. This includes churches and denominations that would not be classified as fundamentalist or evangelical.[2] The leaving and returning age categories of early teens to early twenties are also consistent across denominational lines. If nothing else, this shows that dropping out is an aspect of religious experience in general, rather than the exclusive domain of teenagers and young adults who grow up in evangelical or fundamentalist Christian homes.[3]

Amid all these facts and figures, the point I am happily making is that most leavers come back. Granted, 15 percent of non-returners is 15 percent too many. But parents can be encouraged by knowing that however terrifying and painful the experience of their children's faith rejection is, at least 85 percent of these faith dropouts come back. Put the other way around, this means there is only a 15 percent likelihood of a child leaving and *not* returning to the faith.

Most dropouts return. True, their leaving and returning pattern may be varied in terms of length of departure. And their returning may take different forms. Some people come back to a faith experience more conservative and spiritually zealous than before. Others come back to embrace evangelical doctrines but not evangelical social and cultural environments. They may even choose to affiliate with a different evangelical denomination than the one in which they grew up. But the end result is that most dropouts come back to a genuine experience of faith in Christ and an acceptance of the spiritual values of the homes in which they grew up. I will face the tough truth about dropouts who stay out in the next chapter.

In a moment I am going to tell you the stories of two people who came back. Both of them, a man and woman now in their early thirties, grew up in conservative, evangelical Christian homes. Each rejected the beliefs and lifestyles of their homes and churches. They demonstrated the completeness of their faith rejection by living without regard to the moral, ethical or spiritual standards they had been taught. Yet in their late twenties, they turned again to the Lord, repented of their sin and today are experiencing a vital spiritual life and a firm commitment to Christ.

But before I tell you these wonderful, hope-filled stories, I want to make several general observations about leaving and returning based on the research data as well as my own interviews with dropouts.

Understanding the Facts
About Leaving and Returning

First, it's clear that most spiritual leave-taking happens when people are young. Elementary, you say. But sometimes the force of that simple fact gets lost in the shuffle. So perhaps it should be repeated: The early teens to the early twenties are when serious spiritual breakdown is most likely to occur. The research shows and the testimonies of dropouts confirm that the beginnings of faith rejection are rooted in this time frame. The actual decision to walk away may take place during these years or it may come later, but you'll find the origins of the decision in these early years.

The point is self-evident. While all the years of your children's lives are important, spiritually speaking, what goes on from the ages of thirteen to twenty-one is critical to their faith. In a special way, these are the years that make the difference if you are serious about passing the Christian faith on to your children. This is *the* time to put first things first. Give your children your time and interest. Show them your love. Seek honesty and intimacy. Talk with your kids. Teach and model as best you can what it means to be a Christian.

My second observation is that parents should anticipate the "returning curve" and work with it. We know that somewhere toward the end of college or shortly thereafter, leavers begin to wrestle with some serious practical questions. What about marriage and occupation? Children and family life? These kinds of thoughts turn the philosophical debates of the teen and college years into real life issues and choices.

During this re-evaluation-of-life period, parents can make a special effort to reach out to a son or daughter who has rejected the faith. This is a God-given second chance to reopen the lines of communication and find the family love and intimacy that so many dropouts say they missed when they were younger.

All parents understand how hard it is to communicate with their kids, no matter how good the intentions may be. Perhaps the best approach at this time is simply to be interested in your children's lives. Ask them how they are and really listen. Probe around. Talk. Do things together. Something as simple as going to a ball game or on a family picnic or to the beach. Remind yourself about what you know: No matter what your children are saying and doing, they're re-thinking it all again in their early twenties, especially their faith.

One final comment about the returning curve. If leavers don't come back in their twenties (or if they choose this time to leave), there is yet another time frame that definitively opens the door to spiritual renewal. It's when their own kids turn twelve or thir-teen and start doing in their home what they did in yours. A taste of teenage rebellion, a frightening inci-dent in which their kid gets into trouble with substance abuse or the law, and a thirty-five- or forty-year-old leaver, who remembers something of the stability and sturdiness of the Christian faith in his parents' home, will tend to look again with renewed interest and open-ness at spiritual matters.

Parents can also count on the changed life perspec-tives that come at thirty-five or forty. A little maturity mixed in with some of life's hard knocks will turn hearts toward home and faith. Also, the realization that you aren't going to live forever, which is a universal rite of passage in the middle and late thirties, adds its own quiet but insistent demand to come to grips with life . . . and death.

So there is, in the leaving and returning trajectory, a second and third opportunity to see your children come back to the Christian faith and the values they learned when growing up. Your understanding and patience, as well as your interest and concern for them and their families at this time, are an important aspect of joining forces with the events and ideas that are already at work in your children's lives.

Through all of this, Christian parents are praying and trusting. They know from the Bible that God sees and cares for their wandering children. They lie down to sleep at night confident that the Good Shepherd does not rest even when 99 percent of the sheep are in the fold. Instead, He leaves them safely behind and goes again into the cold, dark night to seek and save one lost sheep.

"Christ, Get Out of My Life"

Ron was one of those lost sheep.

Ron grew up in a Christian home in the Baltimore area and attended an evangelical church with his parents and his sister. He made a conscious commitment of his life to Christ when he was in his pre-teens and was active in his church, local youth ministries and camps as well as a parachurch organization that worked with high schoolers.

From a strategic standpoint, Ron seemed positioned to make it safely through the spiritually critical years. He had home and church encouragement as well as peer support. But there were a few chinks in his armor. He was troubled by his father's materialism and status anxiety which he saw as unchristian. Or he did not understand his faith very well from a theological and intellectual standpoint. That shortcoming would undermine his confidence in his faith during a high school biology course in which his teacher picked on him because she knew he was a Christian. In most cases, he was defenseless in the face of her attacks on his beliefs.

But biology was not Ron's problem. His real difficulty lay in the growing realization that his faith was neither meaningful nor enjoyable. Despite his public ex-

pressions of faith and joy, deep inside he was an unhappy young man who was tormented by the fact that
his non-Christian friends seemed happier and more fulfilled than he.

Slowly and a little uneasily at first, Ron began the
journey away from his faith. Then came a definitive
break in which he decided that he would forsake his
Christian friends and faith and "pursue coolness," as he
put it. "It was a conscious effort," he explained, "to
make those contacts, to develop those relationships, to
get there." Then came the choice to make the break
from Jesus Christ Himself. Listen to Ron's words.

"I remember walking down the halls of my high
school. I had come to the decision that I did not want
Christ to rule my life anymore, that it wasn't fun and I
needed out. I used to be able to walk down the halls of
my high school feeling that I was walking hand in hand
with the Lord, that we were one, walking in step with
each other. I remember as I dissolved that relationship,
feeling and actually seeing in a sense, that Christ was
on my left side and I said, 'Christ, get out of my life.' I
remember it being like a tug of war, like He didn't want
to but I was forcing Him to. Slowly He went back and
up until He finally disappeared out of the roof of my
high school. And He stayed out for seven years."

Ron had some more disconnections to make.

"I had some very close friendships among Christian kids. I just had to cut them off. They weren't
accepted in the cool crowd. I couldn't maintain those
relationships and be in the cool crowd. I think about
those people, three or four of them. I look back and I
miss them. I wish I could find them today and ask their
forgiveness."

Ron never talked about his struggles with his
parents. Nor did he speak with the leaders of his church
or the Christian organizations in which he had been in-

volved. Even though he was emotionally severed from his faith, he played along at home and church, not wishing to create problems for himself. But he was on a slippery slope that would eventually bring him to a place in which his life came apart in every area.

By the time he got to college, Ron was slipping over the edge. He became sexually active. He began to drink excessively, and he used drugs and dealt drugs. By his sophomore year, alcohol and drugs were taking over his life.

"I started getting stoned once a week, then twice a week until it became three or four times a day. By 1980 I was doing coke, quaaludes, speed and acid. I got to the point where I would warm up for parties by doing bong-hits, then a hit of speed, a half a quaalude, then a pint of Seagrams Seven. Then I would go to a party and drink more and smoke more."

Someone has said that it is both a wonderful and terrible thing to be the child of praying parents. To be out of God's will and have their prayers rising to the Father's house daily on your behalf is to invite unpredictable consequences. Unknown to Ron, his parents and grandparents knew he was in dreadful spiritual danger and were praying for him daily. Looking back now, Ron can see that the Lord was trying to get his attention all during this time. But he wasn't looking or listening.

Still, God refused to be shut out of Ron's life. His calls to Ron became louder and more insistent until Ron was forced to hear the Speaking Voice. One night after a party, when he was in a drunken, drug-induced stupor, Ron got into a violent fight in which he came close to doing life-threatening harm to another young man. After that incident, Ron knew his life was out of control.

Not long afterward another event forced Ron to

face the truth about himself. One evening during an on-air shift at a radio station near his college, Ron opened the microphone to speak but could not remember either his name or the call letters of the radio station. His brain would not work and his mouth could not utter coherent sounds. God had gotten through.

Still confused, Ron went to visit a friend for a week. While there, he saw the truth: At twenty-four years of age he was going nowhere but down. He was living a tormented life, not at all like the fun-filled life he once imagined that unbelievers enjoyed. In the quiet of the night he knelt in his room and gave his life back to God. A wandering sheep had come home.

Ron's journey back to a healthy faith was not easy. He had to re-learn and re-understand most of his beliefs. He knew the Bible intellectually, but the real meaning of its truths were tangled up in his confused childhood and teenage understanding of the gospel. But in time, his new understanding of Christ and the Christian life developed into a strong, vibrant faith that today is joyful and full for him and wonderful to behold by others. His life is marked by a visible witness to the saving grace of a merciful God.

"The Things I Learned as a Child Were Still There"

Darlene was also a lost sheep.

Darlene is an African-American, a factor significant to her story because it was the challenges of radical Black students during college that caused her to question her faith and the spiritual values she had been taught.

Born in western Pennsylvania, the second of seven brothers and sisters, Darlene grew up in a middle-class home that was socially traditional and theologically conservative. Her father was the head of the home and her mother was a submissive wife. Her father's strong, domineering personality and her mother's compliant meekness introduced an "X" factor in Darlene's faith journey that eventually would become the central issue regarding her faith.

At some stage in her early life, Darlene decided that if other men were anything like her father, she didn't want to love men. Instead, she preferred women who would love her like her mother loved her. And so, in the complicated mix of the origins of sexual identity, there began a long struggle with homosexual tendencies which finally overcame her and carried her away from the Christian faith of her home and church.

Darlene was a lesbian. I say *was* intentionally. An equally significant part of Darlene's story is her deliverance from homosexual practice and her determination to live not only a disciplined, holy life today but also to seek sexual re-orientation through the help of others who themselves have come out of homosexuality.

Darlene's faith foundations began to shake in college when fellow students pointed out that the Christian faith she was embracing was a White man's religion. It was this faith, they said, that had been used to keep their slave ancestors in subservience. And it was being utilized in much the same way today to oppress Blacks and keep them "in their place." Christianity made no difference in people. White Christians treated Black Christians as prejudicially as anyone else.

Confronted with this intellectual and cultural challenge to her faith, Darlene began to seriously question her beliefs for the first time in her life. Added to her growing struggles with homosexuality, these observations about Christianity by her non-believing peers intensified Darlene's doubts.

Darlene continued to attend church during this time. But when she finished college and moved away from her hometown, she stopped going to church. Her doubts had formed into a conclusion: She wanted to get away from the faith of her home and church. When she made that decision she also came to another conclusion. She would give in to her homosexual tendencies and act upon them, which she did.

Darlene's return to faith came along an unexpected line. In the midst of her growing confusion and pain over her lesbianism, she decided to talk with a campus pastor about her struggles. It was a God-directed choice.

"The Lord just placed her there," Darlene explained with quiet confidence. "Her manner was perfect. She was not forceful or dogmatic. She didn't insist that I must not do certain things. The Lord used her to raise faith issues and questions that I already knew about. That's effective with me because I like to think about things and come to my own conclusions. Had she shaken her finger at me and said, 'You know what the Word says about this,' I probably would have ended up making the wrong decisions as a further act of rebellion."

God was placing another incident into Darlene's life which would become decisive, spiritually speaking. One of her best friends, a male fellow student who had grown up in a similar Christian background, converted to a cult at this time. She knew his choice would affect their friendship. In an effort to persuade him not to convert, Darlene began to read her Bible and then started to study it intensely. "What ended up happening," Darlene says with a wry smile, "was that I wound up persuading myself that the claims of Christ were true.

The end result was that I recommitted my life to Christ."

Darlene's final comments about her return to the Christian faith of her home and church are especially interesting.

"Even when I was doing the worst things, I never really ever threw my faith out entirely. While I had stopped going to church, I never said, 'Jesus Christ, get out of my life.' The things I had learned as a child were still there.

"As I look back, I can see that my mother modeled God's unconditional love. I have never doubted that my mother loved me. My father represented truth to me, no matter what our conflicts were. I've never doubted as far back as I can remember that he said what he meant and he meant what he said. Those two things, love and truth, coming together in my parents, modeled God for me. I'm sure it was a part of the reason I came back to my faith."

In one sense, Darlene's story of return is the same as other stories of wandering sheep who find their way back to the Shepherd's fold. It is a joyful song of deliverance, a hymn of praise to a saving, reconciling God. But from another perspective, her return is special because it shows that even the most difficult and complicated personal problems cannot block out God's love and truth. Homosexuality is just about as confusing as life gets, yet Darlene heard and responded to the Shepherd's call through it all.

Darlene's problems have not disappeared. She still has struggles. Her relationship with her father is not yet fully resolved. Her journey to a new sexual identity is still underway. "Life doesn't automatically fall in place when you surrender yourself to Jesus," Darlene admits. "There are consequences that come from doing things against God's will. Yet I do have the peace of knowing that I am serving God and glorifying Him with my life. It's more than just making it into heaven."

Most dropouts are temporary leavers. And that is the good news.

14

Dropouts Who Stay Out

Some people walk away and never come back.

That is a sentence I wish I did not have to write. I know even the thought that a much-loved child might walk away from his or her faith and not return is extremely painful for the parents, family members and friends of prodigals.

But I have no choice other than to consider this aspect of faith rejection because it's the truth. Some people will leave and not return. To know that and deliberately neglect it is to take an incomplete look at this subject.

The fact that some people leave and do not come back hit home in a personal way during a visit to England a number of years ago. While there, I visited an elderly couple who are distant relatives of mine. I had obtained their names from a cousin who insisted that I stop and see them while I was in England. I'll call them Mr. and Mrs. Smith.

My visit to their home was a special occasion for them and for me. They prepared a lovely meal and invited their family members to attend. Even though we had never met, I sensed an immediate kinship with them. Certain mannerisms seemed familiar. I recognized Mr. Smith's laugh immediately. And after a tour of their back yard, I knew from what side of the family my love of flowers and gardening had come.

The unfamiliar part was the absence of anything overtly Christian. All the other family members I know of in the United States and England are believers. Being with family has always been synonymous with being around people who were openly Christian.

But this was different. Outwardly, the Smith family gave no evidence of Christian belief. No Bibles, no Christian books or mottoes, no prayer of thanksgiving before a sumptuous meal.

As we began to talk, our conversation turned to our family backgrounds. We chatted and laughed as we talked of my father's childhood visits to their home many years ago, including the account of his one-story fall through the floorboards of an out building which I had heard numbers of times in my own home.

Before long, I was asking questions about Mr. Smith's father. I was especially interested in his faith. Was his father a religious man? No, Mr. Smith replied. But his grandfather had been a serious, sober man with fierce Christian convictions and a forceful personality.

"My father left home when he was young," Mr. Smith said. "He wanted to get away from his father and his impossible Christianity. My father hated it."

I was surprised at how much Mr. Smith knew about his father's faith rejection. Obviously, his father had worked out some of his own inner struggles by telling his children about it, however negatively. I also knew from Mr. Smith's detailed description that his father had not walked away and simply forgotten about God. Whatever happened, he continued to wrestle with faith questions long after he made his choice to get away from his father's home and Christianity.

My questions continued. Had his father ever spoken about God in a positive sense? Not that he could remember. Had his father tried to interest the family in religion in any way? No. My host had no interest in religion, nor had he sought to influence his own children or grandchildren in religious matters. That was their business, he said.

Sadness welled up in me. I looked at his handsome grandchildren and thought of their spiritual emptiness and the prospect of a life with little or no attention to God. I thought of my own children who had heard about God from their earliest moments.

Then came dismay as I realized that these distant relatives of mine were living proof that some people walk away and never return, at least so far as external evidence is concerned. Grandfather Smith's decision to reject the Christian faith in which he had grown up had set in motion a chain of events that reached into this dining room in the late twentieth century.

God alone knows the hearts of Mr. Smith and his family. I am not their judge. I often wonder why I was not more direct in my witness to them, more insistent that they consider the claims of Christ in their lives despite their heritage of non-belief. Perhaps I was frightened off by the impact of Grandfather Smith's story. I pray God will yet open a door for me to speak with them about the need to make a decision to receive Christ as their personal Savior.

Parents in Pain

While writing this book, I have thought about Grandfather Smith's father, my distant relative. No one has to tell me that he grieved for his prodigal son. Somehow, I think I know him. I can picture him on his knees, face in hands, crying out to God for his lost boy. I wonder. Did he ever hear his son speak the name of God with reverence? Was there ever any personal or spiritual reconciliation between the two of them? I wish I knew.

Is there greater sorrow for Christian parents than this? Is there a balm in Gilead to heal the wounds of Christian moms and dads who see a son or daughter living with little or no regard for God? Where is God when something like this happens to loving, caring Christian parents? Why does it happen, Lord?

Troubling questions like these linger long after we have read (or written) books analyzing why people from Christian homes leave the faith. In a certain sense, I have tried to answer some of them. But I cannot answer them all, nor can anyone else, including those who are better qualified to offer answers than I.

In his helpful book *Parents in Pain*, Dr. John White begins by titling his first chapter, "It Ain't That Easy." In it he gently but firmly dismantles any idea of employing simple answers for hard questions about parents and prodigals. A few pages earlier in his prologue, he establishes his bona-fides for making this statement by opening the door of his own home so readers can look in.

"We thought we knew our strengths and weaknesses," he says of himself and his wife. "We were modest. Indeed, we were humble. As Christians we talked about our total inability to run our lives apart from God, and we thought we understood what we were saying. Christ would be the center of our marriage. At the same time, with pious naiveté, I imagined that such an intelligent spiritual husband with such a beautiful wife would undoubtedly give rise to four children who would be the envy of parents everywhere.

"As matters turned out it was Lorrie and I who were startled. As the years passed we grew progressively more humiliated and hurt. We little foresaw the day when we would sit in mutual pain, both of us silent because we had nothing left to say."[1]

Easy answers to tough questions? Never. But there are some answers and ultimately there is *an* answer if we are willing to embrace it in faith. There is a God who sees all and knows all, a God who, somehow in some way, is working all things for good for those who love Him and trust in His purposes. There is a God who cares for His own, a God who does not willingly afflict or grieve His children.

I'll talk more about that later. First, let me tell you about a Christian man who walked into my office on business and wound up telling me another story about a grandfather. I'll call him Tim.

Believing Grandfather, Unbelieving Father, Believing Son

After we finished talking about business matters, Tim and I began to talk about our common faith. I knew from earlier comments he had made that he was a serious believer whose desire was to honor and serve the Lord and His people. In fact, he was making plans to leave a successful business and go into full-time Christian service.

Somewhere along the way, Tim mentioned that he did not grow up in a Christian home. In fact, his father was quite anti-Christian and found his son's zeal for the Lord amusing and even irritating. Then came the interesting part. His grandfather, who was no longer living, had been a preacher and a devout, godly man. Christian grandfather, non-Christian father. Sound familiar?

I had been praying that very morning about this chapter in my book. Should I or shouldn't I include a chapter about people who don't come back? I knew this unexpected visit from someone I had never met and which I had not initiated was God's answer to my prayer. I began to probe.

Even though Tim had little or no encouragement to think about God at home and had grown into adulthood as an unbeliever, he began to search for God as a young married man. To my delight and encouragement, he told me that WRBS, the Christian station I manage, had been instrumental in bringing him to a decision to receive Christ as his personal Savior. With a smile, he described how he would sometimes go out to his car to listen so that his family wouldn't know what he was doing. Finally, he decided to give his life entirely to Jesus Christ. From that day forward, his life changed as he began to grow in grace and the knowledge of God's Word.

Today, all of Tim's immediate family members are Christians. He prays for his father and, in whatever ways possible, seeks to show Christ to him, hoping, praying, believing that God will yet get through. What an amazing story. Believing grandfather, unbelieving father, believing son. With tears in his eyes, Tim said he believed his grandfather was among a great host of heavenly witnesses looking down upon him with joy and rejoicing.

It is possible that Tim's dad will yet come to the Lord. I join Tim in praying for that to happen. Unlike Mr. Smith's father who apparently died unbelieving, there is still time for Tim's dad to come to salvation. Perhaps you too could pray for Tim's dad.

I am not saying that this sequence of events was

God's plan for Tim's dad. Nor am I saying that Tim's salvation somehow explains or mitigates his father's unbelief. What is simple and clear in this story, though, is that God is continuing His saving work in this family. He called Tim to the fold and He is still calling to Tim's dad. Just because Tim's grandfather died knowing that his son had rejected the Christian faith does not make that the end of the story. God does not stop working when all seems lost from a human standpoint.

The Bible offers many examples of this. I am thinking of two: Samuel's sons and Josiah, king of Israel.

Faith Rejection Is Not the End

Remember the story of Joel and Abijah, sons of Samuel? Joel and Abijah grew up around the temple, yet they rejected the God of their father. In fact, they were so wicked that the elders of Israel refused to pass Samuel's mantle to them. "You are old, and your sons do not walk in your ways," they said. "Now make us a king to judge us like all the nations" (1 Samuel 8:5-8).

And so Israel got their king and Samuel's sons got the exit door. End of God's dealings with the house of Samuel? No, though Samuel surely must have thought so.

At the beginning of the Eli and Samuel story back in 1 Samuel 2:35, God promised to "raise up for myself a faithful priest . . . I will build him a sure house." This promise was partially fulfilled in Samuel who served God faithfully. Then came the heartbreak of his sons and the transfer of spiritual and judicial authority to King Saul whom Samuel himself was required to anoint. What thoughts went through his mind? What sadness and pain he must have felt. Where was the God of promises?

Had Samuel been able to look into the future, he would have had another perspective. He would have seen God's promise kept for his own household. His grandson, Heman, became a prophet for King David and a "seer in the words of God, to exalt his horn" (1 Chronicles 25:5). Heman's fourteen sons and possibly his three daughters participated in the dedication of the great temple of Solomon (2 Chronicles 5:11-13). Nor was this all.

Several hundred years later, Samuel's godly influence is still seen despite the faith failure of his sons. In 2 Chronicles 35:15, we see the descendants of Heman again involved in spiritual activity, this time in the midst of revival in the nation of Israel.

And so we come to the second of my illustrations, Josiah, the boy-king who went on to become the most godly of all Israel's kings. "Before him," the Scriptures tell us, "there was no king like him, who turned to the Lord with all his heart, with all his soul, and with all his might, according to all the law of Moses; nor after him did any arise like him" (2 Kings 23:25).

Josiah is a story all by himself. He became king at eight years of age (with advisors). He is one of the Bible's most remarkable teenagers (we know his exact chronology from the text) whose only possible match as an adolescent, spiritually speaking, is his own distant relative, King David. He grew into a man who could be compared with the prophet Daniel, spiritually speaking, who was surely influenced by the revival Josiah started. And the verse just mentioned seems to give Josiah the edge when it comes to spiritual standards.

Josiah's story is extraordinary because his spiritual zeal seemed to come from nowhere. His grandfather Manasseh, who reigned for fifty-five years, was one of Israel's most wicked kings of whom it is said that he "seduced Judah and the inhabitants of Jerusalem to do more evil than the nations whom the LORD had destroyed before the children of Israel" (2 Chronicles

33:9). The Scriptures say that "the LORD spoke to Manasseh and his people, but they would not listen" (2 Chronicles 33:10). Finally, God got Manasseh's attention through a military defeat. The old king, humbled and reduced to symbol status, returned to his throne and initiated some spiritual reforms. But by this time, the people of Judah were less than enthusiastic about serving and worshiping God.

Manasseh's son Amon was no better, reigning two years and doing "evil in the sight of the LORD, as his father Manasseh had done" (2 Chronicles 33:22). Amon's fate came at the hands of his servants who killed him in his own house. One can only wonder at the evil of a king whose wickedness is so great his servants rise up and kill him in his castle. Amon was Josiah's father. Ungodly grandfather, ungodly father, godly son.

The Bible says that the people of the land made his son Josiah king in his place (2 Chronicles 33:25). Since he was only eight years old, others ruled on his behalf. Then when he was sixteen he began to be heard from. We read that "he began to seek the God of his father [Jewish for antecedent of any age] David; and in the twelfth year he began to purge Judah and Jerusalem of the high places, the wood images, the carved images, and the molded images" (2 Chronicles 34:3). At twenty years old his heart was set on God. At age twenty-six he began to rebuild the temple and found the Holy Scriptures in the walls which began the sure return to true religion in Judah.

Question. What caused a sixteen-year-old teenager to say to himself one day: "I will seek the God of my fathers"? He had no positive spiritual influence in his family so far as we know. He had no preacher, priest, counselor or teacher of things spiritual. He had no Bible until one was discovered during the rebuilding of the temple (some wise, godly priest knew what he was doing when he tucked those scrolls into the wall and closed them in with mortar). Is it possible that the spiritual influence of Samuel, one of Israel's godliest priests, whose own sons refused to follow God, reached this place hundreds of years after Samuel himself had died in sorrow over the spiritual failure of his children?

In 2 Chronicles 35:15 the name Heman appears among the singers at a Passover ordered by Josiah at the temple. Almost certainly this Heman is the offspring of Samuel whose children were among the singers and musicians at Solomon's temple dedication (2 Chronicles 5:11-13). Surely they were among a godly remnant of people who, despite the decades of evil in Judah, had remained faithful to the true and living God.

As a musician, Heman may have been in the palace and around the boy king for years. Did he sing the songs of David? Did he sing of Jehovah? Did Josiah as child and teenager ask Heman to tell him more about King David and his God? I don't know, but don't say it isn't possible. Samuel may have lost his sons, but he reached his grandchildren. Through them, he may have reached all the way to Josiah and helped instigate one of the greatest revivals recorded in the Bible.

In God's Eyes, Always!

And so we come at last to the one answer about prodigals that I can offer with unshakable confidence. It is the great promise of Romans 8:28: "And we know that all things work together for good to those who love God, to those who are the called according to His purposes." For Christians, all things are working together for good. Somehow, in some way, even a prodigal child results in that which is good. By our standards and in our pain, *never!* In God's eyes, *always!*

There are times and places in our lives when we must get to the bottom of what we believe. Is God in control of things or not? Is He there or is He far away and unconcerned about us? Do we believe Romans 8:28 and the truth of God's sovereignty over our lives? Or do we take this verse as a generalization and say, "Well, I suppose that in most cases things work out for Christians, but not always"?

We intensify our pain and sadness when we waffle over this verse of Scripture. There is no room to maneuver, explain or scheme here. Either God is working all things together for good to those who love Him or He is not. We believe and trust or we do not. If we embrace the truth of Romans 8:28, however daunting a prospect that may be in the face of prodigal children, we go free. We may hurt but we have the peace of God and with it His comfort.

Vance Havner, the remarkable, down-home Christian "philosopher" of yesteryear (who himself was a temporary leaver), wrote these insightful words in 1931:

> Faith does not promise ideal circumstances. It does master every outward condition and move mountains as Jesus said it would, but it changes them by changing us. It builds in us a spirit that no outward condition can bother, and when a man is victorious within, the without does not matter. Objective realities may be what they were before, but the man is different; his attitude has changed and for him that changes everything. It is not things themselves but our way of looking at them that matters. Faith gives him the right perspective, and when he sees things as they really are they lose their terrors.[2]

Recently I was talking with a mother who was concerned about the spiritual struggles of her daughter. The spectre of a prodigal child loomed large in her mind as she said, "I'd rather not have children than see them grow up and reject the Christian faith." I empathize with her and feel her pain. But I disagree with her outlook on her children.

We cannot live in fear or doubt about our children's spiritual destiny. We conceive our children in love and faith, and then we give them to God. We do our best to bring them to Christ and teach them what it means to live as Christians. If we take any other approach we are held captive by the circumstances of life, many of which we cannot control, including our children's free choice to walk away from the Christian faith. Faith in a sovereign God who loves us and intends the best for us is the key that sets us free from the bondage of doubt and fear.

We know what *all* means and we know what *good* means in the context of Romans 8:28. Those are the tough words of this verse when it comes to a son or daughter who is gone from the faith, temporarily or permanently. Sometimes it just doesn't seem possible that God can be at work in these kinds of troubles in the lives of believers.

So I'd like to point to another significant (but under-noticed) word in Romans 8:28 that is equally as important as *all* and *good*. That word is *together*. Taken individually, the events of our lives often appear disconnected from anything good. They are dissonant and unharmonious, like a tenor or bass part of a familiar song sung by itself. Alone, such a part is unrecognizable by everyone, except perhaps the most musically trained and knowledgeable. But when put together with the rest of the piece, these individual parts make sense.

The same is true of unexplainable painful events in our lives. By themselves they make no sense. But joined with the other elements of the story, they begin to take the shape of something "good."

Think of Joseph in the book of Genesis. Grievously lost to his father through the evil actions of his brothers, he endured a series of catastrophes which in themselves were disastrous. But together with all the other events of his life, his troubles became the means of deliverance for himself and his family. The bad was a necessary prelude to the good. Without being thrown into the well he would never have gone to Egypt. Without being falsely imprisoned in Egypt, he would have never been noticed by Pharaoh through whom he became the CEO of Egypt and finally the savior of his own people.

I think most Christians believe Romans 8:28. Our problems come more along the line of how to embrace this verse when life brings us troubles and sorrows too great to bear. The apostle Paul offers us hope and help in our struggles by reminding us that the Spirit helps us in our weaknesses (Romans 8:26). This is the "how to" assistance we need to believe the promises God has given us. He Himself, through His own Spirit, will help us believe His promises.

Let go, Mom and Dad. Give your son or daughter to the Lord. Believe the stupendous promise of Romans 8:28. It is a decision we must all make, whether our children are safely in the fold now or whether they are away. Trusting God completely is the Christian parents' only place of true peace and safety.

Surprise

Sometimes a light surprises the Christian
  while he sings;
It is the Lord, who rises with healing in His wings;
When comforts are declining, He grants
  the soul again
A season of clear shining, to cheer it after rain.

Chapter Fourteen

Though vine, nor fig tree neither,
Their wonted fruit shall bear,
Though all the field should wither,
Nor flocks nor herds be there;
Yet God the same abiding,
His praise shall tune my voice,
For, while in Him confiding,
I cannot but rejoice.

—William Cowper

15

A Conversation With Three Brothers

One of the intriguing questions of faith rejection is how one or two children from the same family can turn away from the Lord while their siblings follow the Lord with relatively little deviation. Same parents, same environment, different results. How does it happen?

The simple answer is that every person is different. We understand our homes, churches, relationships and the Christian faith itself from our own peculiar viewpoint. Whether our parents are consistent or inconsistent, our homes stable or unstable, our churches good, bad or indifferent, people put their own spin on the gospel based on their own perspectives.

These perspectives are shaped by personality and temperament as well as circumstances. A compliant son or daughter is going to respond to Christian teaching differently than a non-compliant child. Parents are going to relate differently with each child no matter how hard they try to be neutral. Unexpected events such as the death of parent or being uprooted and moved to a different state can play a significant role in how children in the same family respond to the Christian faith.

The time frame in which one grows up can also play a major role in faith rejection. I touched on this in Chapter 3 where I sketched out some of the significant changes in American society that have affected Christian families. One can only guess, for example, at how different our culture and our churches would be without television or the widespread infiltration of drugs into American society in the last three decades.

The social revolution of the 1960s and 1970s profoundly affected children born into Christian homes during those two decades as well as the decade prior to that period. The winds of change were pervasive; no one escaped, with the possible exception of closed communities like the Amish. Among evangelical young people of that generation, the potential for faith rejection rose exponentially.

To show how children from the same family can grow up and go different ways, spiritually speaking, I interviewed three brothers. Their stories are representative of Christian families where one or several of the children go fairly straight down the highway (with some side-to-side wobbling), while one or more go entirely off the highway.

My intention is to let the story tell itself. I interviewed each brother separately. In each case, I asked the same questions with a few exceptions based on the need to clarify some answers. The stories of the older brothers are not unusual and will probably sound familiar to many readers. Their observations about the

Christian faith and their home and church experiences are incisive and are very helpful to anyone interested in questions of faith rejection.

The really fascinating part comes when the stories of the non-wandering brothers are placed side by side with their younger brother's frightening account. There are some obvious faith-affecting events and experiences in these stories, especially the youngest brother's. I encourage you to draw your own conclusions.

Most of the facts normally needed to introduce a story like this are woven throughout the brother's comments. I will let you put them together as you go. However, several pertinent facts are not mentioned: This is a middle-class White family, reared mostly in the middle Atlantic region. The brothers were born in 1943, 1945 and 1951.

Jay

Q. Describe your home in general terms and also in terms of your relationship with your parents.

A. Our home was unusual because our father was a preacher and we were always moving around. Today such mobility is fairly common, but in those days it was more unusual. So there was a certain amount of instability just from that.

So far as my parents were concerned, both had come to know the Lord relatively late in life, but they had gotten their feet pretty firmly on the ground spiritually. From the beginning of their marriage they had pursued the study of the Word and had attempted to live a committed Christian life, so we came into a stable situation there. Even though there were some glaring problems in terms of relationships, I can look back and see that they always had a heart for the Lord.

In terms of standards of behavior there was not

much leeway. It was pretty cut and dried regarding right and wrong. We had no doubts about who was in charge or what the hierarchy of authority was. So in that sense we had stability too.

My mother passed away when I was in my middle teens—probably at the time I needed her most. Yet she had already set a good example and had established a foundation for me in quite a few areas of my life which even today I hold to. Even with the loss of my mother, the stability continued because my grandmother, my mother's mother and a Christian, came to live with us, so the same standards and values continued.

Q. What about your father? Did you have an unshakable certainty that he loved you?

A. I guess I did. I never stopped to think about it. That's a difficult question to answer. I would never have said that he didn't love me. Dad wasn't very accessible in terms of relationships. There wasn't much display of affection. But he made efforts to spend time with us, whether it was a picnic or some sports outing. Still, I wouldn't say I had an unshakable sense that he loved me, although I never felt my position in the family was ever in doubt or that I was in any danger of rejection.

Q. Was he consistent in terms of what he believed and how he lived? Could you predict what would happen if you did what was wrong?

A. Yes, though my mother was actually more the leader in those areas. For example, my mother had an absolute insistence that every year we were going to enroll in Bible Memory Association. So we had to memorize Scripture until it was coming out of our ears and we hated it. But we had no choice in the matter. My father saw the value in it and went along, yet when Mom passed away, we were no longer enrolled in BMA. My father was a honest man, but his manner didn't always back up what he said. I think I recognize now, more than then, that he wrestled with the same thing we all do, trying to be as consistent in private as we are in public—or in my father's case, in the pulpit.

Q. Did you ever question your faith when you grew up?

A. I'm not sure exactly what that means. If it means that I actually came to a point of some sort of major decision about following or not following the Lord, I would say that never happened. There have been and there continue to be things that cause me to look more carefully at certain aspects of my faith, with a view not so much to jettisoning my faith but fine-tuning it and continuing to grow in it. But no, I cannot recall ever standing at a crossroads where I could have gone either way regarding the Christian faith.

Q. From a faith standpoint, what did you like most about your home?

A. The thing about our home I liked from a faith standpoint was that wherever there was an opportunity for spiritual nurture or spiritual formation, our parents were very quick to make sure we took advantage of those opportunities. We didn't have daily devotions, but we were always involved in the church, and we went to Christian camp every year from the time I was six years old. Starting at age fourteen, I went for four or five summers to a Bible camp where I was on staff and sat under some of the top Bible teachers in the country.

Q. What did you dislike the most in your home from a faith standpoint?

A. I can't think of much. If there was anything at all, it was probably the unrealistic expectations other people sometimes put on me as a preacher's kid. But that's almost embarrassingly insignificant.

Q. Did you like church? Was it meaningful to you socially, intellectually and spiritually?

A. For the most part, church really wasn't helpful. There was a welcome social aspect in our close-knit youth groups. But otherwise, not much. Actually, I'm not even sure where I stood spiritually until I was about eighteen years old. I prayed to receive the Lord at age six, but there was such a lack of fruit and victory in my life, I'm not really sure if I was a Christian. The fact that I didn't get a lot of benefit from church may have been because I wasn't really open to it.

Q. Did anything trouble you seriously about your faith?

A. No. I think the constant exposure to Christian things from the beginning made a difference, although I know others who had the same kind of Christian childhood who became very troubled about their faith. There are things I struggle with today, including the old question of what is the church. Who are we? What are we about? Why isn't the church delivering the goods? But I was not and am not troubled about things that really touch on the basics of the Christian faith.

Q. What were the circumstances surrounding the "decision" you made at age eighteen?

A. I was at a Bible conference where I had been working for several summers. I had graduated from high school and I wasn't sure what I was going to do, so there was a certain level of dis-ease there. Somehow during that summer as I listened to those Bible teachers, the Spirit of God began to open my eyes to my spiritual inadequacies and failures, and my lack of a future. I think I was having a real Ecclesiastes syndrome—what was life all about?

One particular evening after a meeting, I was walking up and down the road trying to figure out what to do. On that night I said to the Lord, "I'm tired of playing games. I want to be what You want me to be. If I'm not Your child, I want to be."

From that point on, my whole thinking process began to change. My goals all became reoriented. At the end of the summer, I decided to go to Bible school and into Christian service. I went directly into Bible school and on into ministry which included overseas missionary service.

Q. When you think about your childhood and your Christian home from today's perspective, can you think of things that could have been done differently that might have helped you avoid some of these struggles and also would have helped you make an unswerving commitment to Christ from your early years?

A. I think my father's seat of the pants approach to child rearing left me without a lot of substantive, helpful counsel in some of the major areas of my life. I know he was doing the same thing we all do, learning as we go, but it was pretty hands off. I think he wanted to talk, but we never did except for one time when I wanted to drop out of Bible school. He took time with me one day to encourage me to stay in school. I'm sure my kids could say I've dropped the ball too, but I've tried hard through their growing-up years to be interested and available. I wish I had experienced some of that with him, especially on significant issues.

I've tried to think about what happened back then as I was preparing for this interview, and all I can say, and you've heard this before, it's the grace of God. I can't take a checklist and say my parents did this, this and this right, and this, this and this wrong and the good outweighed the bad. If I do that, I can't explain why others had the same kind of Christian childhood and went wrong It had to be the grace of God. I heard someone say once, "If your kids turn out well, don't take too much credit. If they turn out poorly, don't take too much blame."

Peter

Q. Describe your home in general terms and also in terms of relationships.

A. We had a close family in the sense that we did a lot of things together. I felt I had a positive relationship with my parents for the most part, although I felt that I was spanked a lot and that my parents were angry with me a lot of the time. I was an active, strong-willed boy, and I guess I drove them nuts. My older brother and I fought a lot—really up until the end of high school. My younger brother and I always had a good relationship. Basically, I have good memories of our family. Of course, it radically changed when our mother died.

Q. What about your father? Did you have an unshakable certainty that he loved you?

A. Yes. How much of that is retrospective, I'm not sure. I know at the time I felt differently. When my dad spanked me, I would go to my room absolutely furious. I remember feelings of not being loved and being really angry. But with my personality, I couldn't stay angry long so those feelings would go away.

Q. Was your father consistent in terms of what he believed and how he lived? Could you predict what would happen if you did what was wrong?

A. Yes and yes. We knew what to expect. He was frank to a fault.

Q. Did you ever question your faith as you were growing up?

A. I think in the eleventh and twelfth grades I came to a point where I was looking at the church and Christians around me and not seeing what I should see. [Peter lived with his grandmother in his senior year. His father had remarried and moved to another city and gave Peter the option to stay with his grandmother and finish high school.] I didn't reject the Lord as such, but I did enter a phase of my life in which I was often angry about the youth group, the church, whatever, and I let everyone know it.

I think I was put out not so much at God but at the way it was all working out in a practical sense. I could never get away from the reality of God and His truth, but I was angry because I couldn't seem to find anyone who was really a genuine Christian living the way the Bible said. In that context, I really began to think about the reality of my faith and what I actually believed.

In a way this was a kind of faith test, but my doubts and questions never moved me to rebellious acts or anything flagrant. I didn't get into sex, drugs or whatever would typically characterize people who were rebelling against the Lord. I knew deep down that my faith was genuine and I couldn't escape that no matter what was going on around me. Even in my angriest moments, I knew the Lord was real. I think I learned that from both my father and mother. And I believe the Scripture memory I did for many years was an important part of that too. I became a Christian at the age of six and there wasn't a lot of spiritual growth in the next ten or twelve years. But I don't think I ever had a doubt about the reality of the Lord.

Q. From a faith standpoint, what did you like most about your home?

A. I liked the fact that my mom was always there. She didn't work outside the home except briefly at one point. I felt real good about that. Our home was always neat and clean. Our mother baked, made things, sewed us things. I liked that my father took time to play with us, throwing the frisbee, that kind of thing. We went to the ocean together. It all seemed to tie in to the fact that we were a Christian family.

Q. What did you dislike most in your home from a faith standpoint?

A. I can only speak in retrospect about that. I don't think I was analytical or reflective enough when I was younger to see that something was wrong or missing.

As I look back today, though, I think there was too much law. But that was what my parents were taught. My dad was in a very conservative denomination and that was Christianity to him—things you don't do. It wasn't overbearing, but it was there. I think it was probably more of my mother's influence than my dad's because after she died, he shifted away from that emphasis.

My parents fought openly sometimes, and I found those conflicts destructive. There was some unhappiness in their relationship, and it made a real impression on me. There was a hush-hush attitude toward sex. That bothered me and drove me to magazines like *Playboy* to find out more about women. That brought me tremendous guilt, although my dad dealt wisely with me about that by telling me that "those kinds of books" will give you the wrong idea of what women are like.

Q. Did you like church? Was it meaningful to you socially, intellectually and spiritually?

A. It was my social life. My parents had the idea that most unbelievers were pretty bad folks so you shouldn't spend too much time with them. So we spent our time with Christians. I was in youth groups, vacation Bible school, those kinds of things. As a kid I loved that. I found church very boring when I got into my early teenage years, but I figured that was my problem. The adults seemed to find it interesting. I came to a point where I asked if I could stay home Wednesday nights, but my dad made me go.

When I got over the boring part, I was able to find parts of church that I enjoyed—choir, youth group. The thing that really began to trouble me in my junior and senior years in high school was feeling that something was missing in church. I felt like an alien inside the church, although a lot of that was my fault because I was an opinionated, strong-willed kid. But I really was looking for love, for someone to care about me.

Q. At some point in your teen years, did you make a specific decision to live for Christ?

A. I see three phases in my Christian life. At age six I distinctly remember sitting around a campfire at a Christian camp and hearing John 3:16. It really penetrated my heart and I received Christ that night. I have no doubt about that. It's clearly etched in my memory.

And then there was this period we've just been talking about—the church and my struggles. But throughout those years, the Lord never let me alone. I know the Lord had His hand on me.

Then came the third phase. During my first semester in Bible college, I got myself into some serious trouble and for the first time in my life I faced myself. One night in a prayer room on campus, something like Pentecost happened to me. For the first time in my life, I came to grips with who Jesus Christ really was in terms of His majesty and His person. His worthiness to be worshipped hit me like a bombshell. I was completely broken. It was like learning a new language in one second. It was the turning point. Once that happened, I knew that I had found the will of God and could go free to follow Him. It was an unusual thing that I still can't explain other than by pointing to the reality of Christ in me.

Q. When you think about your childhood and your Christian home from today's perspective, can you think of things that could have been done differently that might have helped you avoid some of your struggles and would have helped you make an unswerving commitment to follow Christ from your early years?

A. I think the emphasis on the law undermined the gospel. I had the distinct impression that the Christian life was what you did or didn't do. The concept of Christ living within me, of being a new creation in Christ, was lost somewhere. I became preoccupied with my sin nature rather than Jesus Christ, and that was very destructive to my Christian experience. I felt very guilty most of the time. I think that approach to the Christian faith was a bill of goods. It was a false Christianity that did not draw attention to Christ but rather to self and sin and works.

From my perspective now, I can see it was not an attractive Christianity and that played an important part in my disillusionment with church and the Christian faith during those teen years. I couldn't break free from it. I think that the saving grace in all of it was the good relationship I had with my dad. He loved the Lord with all his heart and he read the Bible. He had his faults and I could see them. But he was genuine. He was real. So even though I was disillusioned with the brand of Christianity he taught, I couldn't get away from the fact that my dad was real because Christ was real. If he had been a phony, I think I would have been long gone.

John

Q. Describe your home in general terms and also in terms of relationships with your parents.

A. I guess I see a couple of different homes, particularly because my mother died when I was eight. The few recollections I have of my mother are neutral. I remember being disciplined by her a lot, but that is not a strong negative impression. She did motherly things and she was there. I really felt her absence when she was gone.

The next "home" was when my grandmother, her mother, came to live in our home for a couple of years. There was no intimacy with her or with my father. He did things with me—we played catch and frisbee—and some of my friends envied that. But there was no real intimacy. I missed that. I guess that was the third "home" part of my childhood.

Q. What about your father? Did you have an unshakable sense that your father loved you?

A. Yes. He showed that basically by trusting me. There were certain things we weren't allowed to do, but there was a lot of trust and he let me make decisions. I felt comfort in that.

Q. Was he consistent in terms of what he believed and how he lived? Could you predict what would happen if you did what was wrong?

A. I hear your question and I see a two-sided answer. There were strong convictions you could depend on, but also a certain amount of uncertainty because he had a temper. There were minor transgressions that were often overlooked and then he would explode about them. At other times, the least little thing would set him off when I didn't expect it. I really feared him. We never really communicated about things, and there were some things I could never discuss with him.

For example, one time I was really excited by a book about revitalized faith and discipleship. My dad, being from a very conservative seminary, took a brief look at it and threw it across the room. He said, "It's faith plus nothing, and I don't want to hear any more about it." Then another time, he came into my room when I was listening to a record, sat on my bed, took the record off, smashed it over his knee and said, "This is trash," and walked out of the room. That kind of behavior produced uncertainty in me and led to a fear of never being sure what might happen.

Q. Did you ever question your faith as you were growing up?

A. There were periods of rebellion, but I'm not

sure those were doubts or a questioning of my faith. My real doubts came in college, which I can talk about later.

Q. From a faith standpoint, what did you like most about your home?

A. That's hard to say. It's hard to separate relationships from faith. I really can't think of anything I liked about my home from a faith standpoint. Maybe as we talk something will come to my mind.

Q. What did you dislike most in your home from a faith standpoint?

A. Hypocrisy. For example, I remember my parents talking around the table about what they didn't like about someone who was making trouble in the church. My stepmother would say, "Well, we love them in the Lord." I remember thinking that meant, "We really hate them." That bothered me.

I didn't like being a PK. We had to do things other kids didn't. We had to sing or play instruments or recite Scripture. It was like we were performing and something in me rebelled against it. We had to do or say something whether it was genuine or not. I guess I felt put in a box.

Q. Did you like church? Was it meaningful to you socially, intellectually or spiritually?

A. Definitely not intellectually. One problem with church was how much we moved around. We were never at a church long enough to develop relationships.

I enjoyed some of the youth groups when I was very young. We did things together and just had fun. I enjoyed covered dish dinners and having fun with my friends afterwards. As a child, I can see those as an important part of my church life. But it wasn't consistent in all the different churches.

Q. You mentioned your real doubts and troubles with your faith started in college. What happened?

A. When I was a senior in high school, I was praying and seeking the Lord's guidance regarding college. I narrowed it down to two Christian liberal arts colleges because I wanted to go into pre-med. I chose the college where I thought God wanted me.

I was a good football player in high school and college and lettered in both high school and college. I ended up being a starter as a freshman in college. During this time I became very good friends with a girl who was a cheerleader. She came from a respected Christian family, but she was a real rebel. She liked to drink beer so when I was with her it became a issue. I'd never really thought about it that much. I knew we weren't supposed to, but when confronted with it, I thought, *What difference does it make?* So I drank beer with her because she liked it and I liked her.

In my sophomore year, I met another girl at the college who was really into partying and drinking, and it wasn't long before I developed a taste for harder stuff—brandy and things like that. The college was very strict, very legalistic, and they had no idea what was going on with this party faction of students.

This same girl was into drugs—speed, hallucinogens—but not shooting up or anything. I remember one night she had some speed and she offered me some. I thought, *This could be fun,* so I took it. It wasn't escapism for me as much as it was a heady thing. I enjoyed the strange crystal clarity I got mentally. I really liked sitting around shooting the breeze when I was high.

That was when I really started becoming a different person. A change of mind came with smoking grass and doing hallucinogens. I became a real creep and started living a debauched life. It wasn't like I was sitting back thinking, *I'm going to trash my upbringing.* It was more like I happened into it. It was just, "Why not?"

I wish I could say that I came to a point where I sat down one day and said, "I'm out of here," because then it would all make sense to me. But it wasn't that way. I just had no reason for *not* doing those things. I enjoyed them. And for once, I had found something meaningful—a group of friends who I had a lot of fun being with. It was all very enjoyable, until the very end when the horrible things started to happen.

Q. As you look back now, what do you think could have been a reason *not* to do these things? What belief or conviction or point of view or anything else could have stopped you from taking that path?

A. I think if I would have had my life more together that I would have chosen a different group of friends. I wouldn't have been attracted to the counter-culture types or stayed with them once I saw what was going on. Strangely enough, I continued to go to church on and off during this time, and I had no problem with that. But I didn't have the emotional support, the inner sense of home and family that would have made it much harder for me to go with the friends I chose.

Now, I see very clearly that—and this is hard to convince people about—Satan uses drugs and alcohol to get a grip on people. Drugs especially. They opened my life up into an occult area and Satan got a hold on me that I was never able to break until there was prayer and fasting by my brothers later on when I was in such a bad state.

I was not responsive to doctrines or rules saying that what I was doing was wrong. Maybe that's just me. But knowing that God is grieved with such behavior and that Satan is trying to get hold of my soul through it, now that's something I respond to. Strange as it seems, I remember times when I would defend the faith from a rationalistic standpoint while this all was going on. I remember saying to people who were making fun of Jesus or criticizing the Bible, "It never worked for me, but I know there are people out there it works for."

Q. How far did you go before you hit the wall? What happened that turned you around?

A. My life was out of control. Amazingly, I was still getting good grades, but I had lost control of myself. I was getting into trouble on campus. In fact, I was the ringleader of a group of guys and girls who did some pretty ugly stuff. Somehow the dean of the school got on to me and I was confronted with getting kicked out of college. I told the Lord if He would get me out of this jam, I would straighten out. And a miracle of sorts happened, because for the first time in the school's history the dean's decision to kick a student out was overturned by a board of appeals. So I stayed in school, but I went back on my promise to God. After that, I really started getting into drugs.

At the beginning of the next semester, I took some scholarship money and started to deal drugs. Being the entrepreneurial type, I decided I was going to get my school bills paid and have some money to play with. So I went to a nearby town during a big rock concert and started selling the stuff openly, like a street vendor. The long and the short of the story is that I ran into a narc and he busted me. This was an Our Town, USA, kind of place, and they saw me as a hardened drug dealer come to town to ruin their kids. They threw the book at me.

I spent more than three weeks in jail waiting for bail. After the first week or so, I remember looking down at a Gideon's Bible in the jail cell on a Sunday morning and thinking, *Gee, I used to go to church on Sunday mornings.* Then the question started to sink into my thick head, "Where am I headed? I'm a pre-med student, and I'm in jail for selling drugs." I picked up the Bible and started reading. As I began to read—and it didn't take long—I came under great conviction and fell on my knees in the cell and cried out to the Lord and said, "This is the pits. I know I'm a real mess." And He heard me.

There is a lot of God's grace in this because even though I called out to the Lord, I still didn't get things right immediately. But He kept the pressure on. I got out of jail but I had a trial date in six months and then I was put on probation. And through that series of events, changes began to appear in my life. I'm still not sure exactly what happened other than the Lord did His work in me, because the change in my life was not just a matter of my resolution to straighten out. The only thing I can say is that someone must have been praying. My brothers and I sometimes talk about all of that and conclude that my praying grandmother was the real explanation. My father had no idea of what was happening, although he knew something was wrong in my life. My brother Peter was praying intensely for me at this time too.

Q. Despite all that you went through, I could probably find a hundred parents who would gladly take the outcome of your story. Here you are, despite the detour, a spiritually strong, mature Christian. You acknowledge the grace of God and the prayers of your grandmother and brothers, along with the sovereignty of God. But is there anything else? Can you put your finger on something—anything—in your home and childhood that may have played a significant part in your return to the Lord?

A. I cannot say with conviction that any particular aspect of my home or Christian upbringing played that role. I've tried to analyze it and I can't. But knowing what I know about Scripture and the promises of God, I can point to the large amounts of Scripture that I had to memorize when I was growing up, especially under my mother's influence. I did that through the third grade. I can also point to the continual exposure to biblical concepts in our home during my formative years —Christian camps, Sunday school, kids programs. I knew a lot about God and what He expected.

The interesting part of all this is that the faith things I learned all along the way, which I didn't like, somehow clicked in my life and I became comfortable with them. "Bring up a child," that sort of thing. Maybe that's the point. Whatever happens in your life, when you're raised in a Christian home you've got God's truth in here. Eventually it surfaces and pulls you back. You actually want it.

Q. When you look back now and consider your home and childhood faith, what do you think could have been done differently that would have made a significant difference in your faith struggles?

A. I wish that my dad would have talked with me about issues of all kinds, faith and otherwise. I remember once when my stepmother found some pornography in my room, he came to me with some Scripture verses and told me to read them. He said if I had any questions that I should talk to him about it. But we never did talk about it. I don't think he knew how. I know his father didn't talk with him. So I can understand that and forgive him for it. But at the same time I regret it. I'm trying very hard to do things differently with my kids in that regard.

• • • • • • • • • • • • • • • • • • •

16

A Conversation With Two Parents

"We wanted him to know that no matter where he went, no matter what he did, he couldn't get away from our love. We were coming at him with love."

Most parents of prodigals endure their sorrows in painful silence. They pray and trust God. But mostly, they deal with their special problem by not talking about it.

These parents are silent because of the guilt, shame, self-doubt, grief and anger that come with the territory. To bring up the subject with anyone, including family and friends, is to tear off the thin layer of healing that forms each day and to pour salt into the reopened wound.

We who watch from outside this circle of pain are also silent because we understand these feelings instinctively. We're afraid of them. We don't know what to say. We offer brief words of encouragement, a pat on the back and our assurances of prayer and support. These are welcome and right. But for the most part, we too say very little about prodigal children.

The outcome of this uneasy silence is that it prevents parents of prodigals, those brave, weary, anguished souls, from doing the one thing they need to do most: share their burden with others. Going through this most difficult experience alone accomplishes little more than intensifying the emotional trauma of it all.

In the conversation that follows, you will see how one couple endured their own painful silence until at last their willingness to open their hearts and lives to their friends brought help and healing to themselves and to others. The unfortunate part of this story is that these parents lived three years with their sorrow until an event in the life of their prodigal son forced them to decide whether they would continue to remain silent or tell all.

You will also learn how these parents managed to live with a semblance of normalcy during this time, even though they were tormented daily, even hourly, by the total rebellion of their son Sean. And you will learn how God in His mercy and grace brought their son home to them.

Admittedly, this story is one-sided. I have not talked with Sean. Someday I hope to hear what happened from his side of the fence. I have no doubt that at some point and in some unlikely way he heard the tender voice of the Good Shepherd calling him back to the fold. Like multitudes of lost sheep before him, he responded to that loving call and went home to the Father's house.

This is the story of John and Becky and their family, two sons and a daughter. Christian parents now in their middle forties, John and Becky's lives were forever changed by a prodigal son whom they could not control from the time he was twelve years old. During this time, John worked in a parachurch ministry while Becky was employed part time in a secular occupation. Today the family, including Sean, his wife and their baby, live in a large eastern city.

As in the case of my interviews with the three brothers, I will let the story speak for itself.

Q. Can you folks sketch in the background of the story for me?

John: Our son was a model child. By the time he was two-and-a-half, he had memorized twenty-six verses of Scripture. He went through various youth programs and typically won awards for being the best student or whatever the goal happened to be. He attended a Christian school and was always a model student.

But when he entered seventh grade, he began to change. The change came when he teamed up with some friends who were interested in other things than school. I think these friends convinced him that sin had more to offer than following the Lord.

Becky: He was physically very mature for his age.

John: Yes, he was bigger than most of the other students. The friends he began to hang around with were also large for their age.

Q. When did you begin to understand that Sean was having problems? What kinds of things started happening?

John: The first indication of trouble was an attitude problem. He didn't want to listen to us. He challenged us. He got into rock music. I remember finding one tape of a group called "The Sex Pistols" which I confiscated. He began to steal things. He was picked up for shoplifting when he was twelve.

Becky: It wasn't that he needed money. He had a paper route and had money in his pocket when he was picked up by the police.

Q. How did you react to these problems and the resistance you were feeling from him?

John: We told him we didn't like what he was doing. I tried corporal punishment at first, but gave up on that. We took away privileges. That slowed him down a little but basically he maintained his belligerence and independence.

By the ninth grade he was beginning to run away from home. He would just disappear for periods of time. Sometimes we would wake up at night and discover that he was gone. One night, when he was fourteen or fifteen, he stayed overnight with a girl and probably became sexually active at that time.

Becky: He would just disappear. That was one of the hardest things. We never knew what to expect next. One minute he was in the house, the next minute he was gone. He would take our car and drive around even though he didn't have a license. One night he went to a friend's house and drank a whole bottle of vodka with Coke. He was so drunk he couldn't do anything.

In the ninth grade we decided to change schools. We sent him to another Christian school which didn't work out. Then in the tenth grade we sent him to a tech school thinking he might be challenged by the change in educational emphasis. He immediately found the worst kids in the school. We learned later that he wasn't even going to classes. He would go in the front door and out the back door with his new friends and go smoke pot. He didn't make it through the semester. He was out of control.

John: He made his getaway at this time. He stole our van and took off with some girl friends. We called the police and we were able to find out who the girls were. That evening we called our church and asked them to pray for Sean in prayer meeting that night.

Becky: That was the first time we told anyone we were having trouble with Sean. It was just too hard to tell people about it.

John: The next day we were in pretty bad shape. I kept reminding Becky about James 1 where we're told to count it all joy when troubles and testings come. It didn't work very well. We weren't counting anything joy.

That day we got perhaps a half-dozen phone calls from people at church. We were surprised to hear how many other people were having problems like this with their kids. In fact, the pastor's sister had rebelled and had turned her back on the Lord and the church. We never knew it until that day. Those phone calls helped a lot. We felt the comfort of friends and the Lord.

That Saturday night at about 10:30 we got a call from the police saying they had picked Sean up in Florida. He was in jail, charged with grand theft auto and being a fugitive. I didn't know what to do. I was on the phone with the police and others for a couple of hours, trying to figure out whether I should go down there or what.

On top of this, I was supposed to preach the next morning at a church in Philadelphia. My message, which I had already prepared, was on Luke 15 and the

Prodigal Son. I remember sitting up there on the platform Sunday morning wondering if I should admit that
I had a prodigal. Then I wondered if that would dis-
qualify me from preaching because it would prove that
I didn't fulfill 1 Timothy 3 that says a bishop should
have his own children under control. I'm sitting up
there arguing with myself: Should I do it? Should I not?
I knew I wanted to describe what the father felt. So I
did it.

What surprised me was that afterwards at the door
of the church when I was meeting the congregation, I
guess twenty to twenty-five people came to me and
said, "I've been through that same thing myself," or
"My children are in the same place as your son is right
now." Opening my heart increased my opportunity to
talk with people about it.

The Lord used that morning in many ways. Later,
I was able to talk with a Christian young man who was
on trial for attempted murder. He knew about Sean and
he was willing to open up and talk to me about himself
because he knew about our troubles. He knew we
didn't have our act together either. He had never
shared anything with anyone before. I see that in many
places now. People who are hurting sense they can
open up to me.

Q. Were you dialoging with Sean at all during this
time? What were you saying to him?

Becky: I was always saying to him, "Sean, when
are you going to change? This is so hard on me." I can't
describe how I felt. During his rebellion things just got
worse and worse. I was talking to a pastor and I said,
"I'm ashamed to tell you this, but I wish the Lord
would take him. I can't stand the pain anymore."

John: Sometimes he would respond positively to

what we said. He would feel bad about what he was doing. But it didn't make much difference for long.

Q. What role did your faith play in your pain? How did it mix in with what you were going through?

Becky (crying): I would be able to deal with it for a while, then it would all come crashing down when Sean would disappear and we didn't know what was happening, whether he was dead or alive. But somehow the Lord got us through. John kept saying, "In everything give thanks." As a mother I can tell you the Lord was good. John helped me so much by constantly reminding me that the Lord is faithful.

God would bring different people into our lives to help us. Once I talked with James Dobson at a banquet. We didn't speak for more than a minute and in that brief moment he encouraged me so much. He said, "I want you to know that you will make it through and that your son will come back to the Lord." I don't know how he could say that. He isn't a prophet, but he said it and it came true.

Q. Did you have feelings of guilt and failure while this was going on?

Becky: Oh yes. You wonder what you did wrong. You think about how you might have done things differently, how you might have changed this or that so that things wouldn't have happened this way.

John: I kept asking myself, "Did I spend enough time with him?" When I looked at it closely, I realized that I spent more time with Sean than my other children. All kinds of questions kept going through my mind. One thing that helped me was the thought that God Himself had prodigal children. Adam and Eve were prodigals.

Q. After you brought Sean back from Florida, did you see any changes in him? Did that experience sober him at all?

John: He was still out of control. He kept running away, sometimes for days. He would steal our money, get the keys to our car and take off. He went to New York once and to a couple of other places. We couldn't handle him. One time he jumped out of the second-story window and ran away.

Becky: It was at this time that my brother offered to take him in. Sean had been through four schools and he was still fifteen years old. We knew we couldn't handle him so we sent him to my brother. He lasted three weeks in school there and after three months my brother sent him back to us.

John: So then we put him into a home for problem kids. It wasn't openly Christian but it was run by Christians. We were really impressed with the place. After a month or so we went away for a little vacation, to get some rest, and we got a phone call: Sean had run away from the home. When we talked to them they said they wouldn't take him back. They said they couldn't do anything with him. So we had to take him home.

At that time I decided to write a contract between us. I told him he couldn't come back unless he signed it and kept his part: no drinking, drugs, running around. I told him, "This gives me permission to put you out of this house if you break this contract." And he said okay.

Becky: We couldn't go anywhere. I literally stayed home all the time. I home schooled him. I hardly went out of the house for a year.

John: We kicked him out three times that year. That was a pretty rough year. He threatened to commit suicide if we didn't let up on him. Then came a break. One of his best friends, a girl, who was just as rebellious as Sean, gave her life to the Lord. She became a ball of fire for God. She went overseas on a summer missions trip and just completely turned around. Sean didn't know what to do.

One night things got pretty bad. We threatened to put him out and he became extremely frightened. He didn't want to go. He was petrified. We found out that he was into witchcraft and the occult. He was hearing things and seeing things in his room.

We called our pastor who immediately suspected occult activity. He came over and began to question Sean. As it turned out, someone had given our son an occult name and had sworn him to secrecy, saying he would die under a curse if he ever told anyone. It took three hours to get that name out of him. Once he said it, he knew the curse wasn't true. He was so relieved to get out from under that.

One time he got high on LSD at an event specifically for Christian kids. When he came home he was incoherent. We sat up all night reading the Bible to him. It was an interesting time to say the least.

He struggled through school and finally graduated a year late. The night he turned eighteen he was gone. It was about that time he started going with this girl. He was drinking and hanging around with her all the time. He would come to our house late at night to sleep if he came home at all. He never ate with us.

One day Sean and this girl came to our home and told us she was pregnant. My first reaction was to tell them they shouldn't necessarily get married just because she was pregnant. We talked about their options but nothing seemed to come of that conversation.

A couple of months later they came over and said they wanted to get married. At first we weren't sure if we wanted any part of it. Then we decided this was a unique opportunity to show our love to both of them. So we decided to be a part of it and do it up right. We rented a fancy place, had the wedding and put together a beautiful reception. All our relatives came. You can imagine what that was like to have a wedding for your son and his bride who was seven months pregnant.

Things got a little better after that. Sean's wife couldn't understand why we treated them so kindly. We tried to help them in different ways. She started coming to our church and brought Sean and the baby with her. Slowly but surely Sean and I started talking more. One night we were talking and out of the blue Sean said to me, "Dad, I led my wife to the Lord." I was speechless.

I'm not sure exactly what happened to Sean during this time, but somehow he got himself right with God and the same day or the next day led his wife to Christ. He never talked to us about it until after it happened. He still hasn't told us the details.

As I look back now, I realize that the day he got things straightened out with God was *four years to the day* from when he got picked up in Florida and put in jail. I don't know if there is any connection, but that is an amazing fact. From the day he told me about leading his wife to the Lord, things have turned around completely. He has been a total joy to us.

Becky: It's been unbelievable.

John: He comes over to our house now and he's the delight of the place. He and his wife come to our house church one night a week. His wife knows literally nothing about the Bible and she loves to study with us. They're totally interested in spiritual things. The Lord is making up for all the pain in a hurry.

Q. As you look back, what do you think was the wisest thing anyone ever said to you as you were going through that experience? Was there anything in particular that was said that helped you handle the pain and suffering and trauma of it all?

Becky: For me, it was John who kept saying, "In everything give thanks," and, "Count it all joy." In all the tears and pain, which no one really understands until they've been through it, those verses held me up.

I was also helped a lot by a woman who told me that she couldn't guarantee that Sean would come back, but she could guarantee that through it all I would become a stronger person who would someday help others. Then she told me her son had done the same thing and was still away from the Lord. She said it was the first time she had ever told anyone. She really helped me by saying I would live through it. Let me tell you, at that time I wondered if I would. You feel like you're going to die of a broken heart. I can't tell you how hard it was. So many tears, so many nightmares, so many times when you're frightened to death.

John: Some friends really helped me too. One guy in a pastoral ministry sat me down and said, "The same thing happened to us when our son was fifteen. The greatest mistake I made was not telling anyone about it. I just kept it quiet." He encouraged us to share our burden with others.

A lot of people told me they were going to pray for Sean every day. In that church in Philadelphia, where I first went public about Sean, there were at least twenty-five people who promised me they would pray for him *every* day. That was so encouraging, just knowing that we weren't in this alone.

My parents stood behind us. They were not shocked or negative about the fact that our son—their grandson—was so messed up.

Becky: That was so encouraging.

John: My father said in a kind of quiet way,

"Sometimes young men have to go their own way to learn what God wants to teach them." That was surprising for me because he never had any prodigals in his family. I don't know how he knew to handle it that way.

Q. Have you got anything to say to parents of prodigals?

John: I would say there is hope. All kinds of hope. God is at work in your child's life. He can use the strangest things to convict kids, to get into their thinking.

Becky: You've got to let your prodigal children know that you still love them no matter what happens. I think that's the one message that got through to Sean. We were constantly telling him, "We hate what you're doing, but we love you, Sean, and we'll go right on loving you, even though you reject us and the Lord."

John: We wanted him to know that no matter where he went, no matter what he did, he couldn't get away from our love. We were still coming at him with love.

That night the Florida police called me, they asked me if I wanted to talk with him and I said yes. They said, "Here he is," and handed the phone to him. I said, "Sean, I want you to know that I love you and I have forgiven you for what you've done. I want to help you in any way I can."

I didn't feel like saying that, but I knew it was the truth and I just chose to be like the father in Luke 15. Sean's response was negative. He said, "Oh yeah." His response was still negative even when I picked him up at the jail. Despite your child's reactions and your feelings, you choose to do and say what you know is right.

Q. Any final comments?

John: One of these days I'd like to go to that church in Philadelphia where all those people prayed for Sean. I'll have him with me but not tell them. Then I'll have him play, "Jesus Loves Me" on the piano for special music and just before I begin to preach, I'll say, "By the way, before I get into my message this morning, someone here wants to say something." Then Sean would come up and stand in front of that congregation and say, "I'm Sean. I want to thank all of you for praying for me."

• • • • • • • • • • • • • • • • • • •

17

*The Speaking
Voice*

Surprises. I had a few during the course of researching and writing this book.

The high rate of return among known dropouts surprised me. I began my research thinking that more people stayed out than came back, but I was to learn that most people come back. What a nice surprise that was.

I also found the consistent dropout rates across denominational lines intriguing. Somehow I had assumed that the rigorous standards of belief and behavior that are integral to evangelical Christianity would predispose people who grew up in that environment to a higher dropout rate. It's always harder to live up to tougher standards. But it isn't so. People drop out of mainline churches and even fringe religious groups at about the same rate as evangelical churches.

Of all the things I learned, however, nothing surprised me more than a truth I already knew but had placed off to the side in my "given" category. My surprise was not so much in learning or even relearning this truth, but in having it emphasized so much that it took on a new and fresh dimension in my thinking.

This re-emphasized truth is that God is *everywhere* and that He is *always seeking* His own. Walking away from your faith is not simply a matter of washing your hands of God and all you have learned about Jesus Christ and the Christian life. You cannot simply decide that you want a different way of life that involves little or no regard for God and His eternal truth. It's not that easy.

King David spoke about this in Psalm 139:7-12 where we see him pondering the great truth about the God who is everywhere:

> Where can I go from Your Spirit? Or where can I flee from Your presence? If I ascend into heaven, You are there; if I make my bed in hell, behold, You are there. If I take the wings of the morning, and dwell in the utter-most parts of the sea, even there Your hand shall lead me, and Your right hand shall hold me. If I say, "Surely the darkness shall cover me," even the night shall be light about me; indeed, the darkness shall not hide from you, but the night shines as the day; the darkness and the light are both alike to You.

There is no escape from the God who is everywhere. He is there and He is ceaselessly calling His own back to the Father's house.

In his wonderful little book *The Pursuit of God*, A. W. Tozer says that "God is forever seeking to speak Himself out to His creation."[1] The entire Bible, says Tozer, supports the idea that God is continuously speaking to us: "Not God spoke, but *God is speaking*. He is by His nature continuously articulate. He fills the world with His speaking voice."[2]

This simple Bible fact of the ever-present, ever-seeking God forced itself upon me as I talked with dropouts who had come back to a renewed faith. Over and over they said the words until at last in my dullness I heard them: "God never let me alone." "God kept putting roadblocks in my way." "I didn't see Him at the time, but now I can see God was trying to get my attention." "God kept trying to reach me and I wouldn't listen. He finally had to hit me over the head with a baseball bat."

I also learned that God speaks in many different ways to these dropouts. Unknown to an angry and rebellious young woman, God is revealing Himself in a beautiful, color-splashed Maryland springtime. He is there in a dazzling clear, star-filled November night in the Sierra Nevadas. He speaks when a baby is born or dies. He shouts in drug busts and drunken brawls. In accidents and incidents, in happenings and happenstance, God is calling His wandering children to Himself.

It does not matter that these wanderers refuse to listen or that they will not attend church or that they become silent when the conversation turns to spiritual things. It does not even matter if they refuse to read the Bible or pray. What matters is that they cannot escape from the God who is everywhere and who is always speaking.

This great, omnipresent God also speaks through the Scripture verses and a thousand lessons learned in childhood at home and church, all of which are carefully stored in the human computer we call the brain. God, who designed this amazing organ, knew from the beginning that He could communicate through these never-lost truths, even when they had been consciously rejected by His rebel creatures. It happens. Over and over, dropouts who have come back will tell you the same story.

Let me tell you about two dropouts who couldn't get away from the Speaking Voice.

"I Was Given Another Chance"

Trish was fourteen years old when her parents found Christ as their personal Savior. Their conversion was dramatic and entirely life changing. What was once permitted in their home—drinking, partying and dancing—came to a screeching halt. Trish's fun-and-games routine ended along with other activities she enjoyed with her friends. She went from being in the middle of the action to being an outsider looking in.

Needless to say, this new way of life made little sense to Trish. Even after she made a profession of faith in Christ, she chafed under the new rules and regulations. It wasn't long before a major conflict erupted between Trish and her parents. The outcome was a classic case of teenage rebellion followed by Trish's departure from home even before she finished high school.

Bitter about God and disillusioned with Christianity, Trish went her own way, crashing through life without regard to her family or the Christian faith she had learned at home and church. She went deep into the drug culture; her life consisted of drinking and partying. She spiraled downward toward death. Her boyfriend died in her arms of a self-inflicted gunshot wound. She committed murder (by her own admission) when she aborted her unborn baby.

But God was there, calling, speaking. Listen to the details of how He was trying to get Trish's attention.

"My father never stopped praying for me," she

said. "Wherever I went, I kept meeting Christians. Two people connected with the bank where I worked were Christians and were praying for me. My cousin became a Christian during this time and began witnessing to me. I couldn't believe how many Christians were coming into my life."

Trish still wasn't listening. Then came the day when she heard God speak. Was it in church or at a Christian meeting? Was she tuned to Christian radio or a Christian television program? No. Trish wouldn't give God a whisper of a chance to reach her along those lines of communication. Instead, she was watching the *Oprah Winfrey Show*. The subject of the program? Demon possession—something that had fascinated Trish as she moved along the edges of the drug subculture.

"I really didn't believe in hell or Satan from a personal standpoint," Trish admitted. "Then a priest [on the program] who had witnessed exorcisms said, 'Satan hates humans because they're created in God's image and his ultimate objective is to destroy them.' Then a woman shared her testimony about how she had been possessed by a demon and had tried to kill her baby. She was freed through the power of Jesus Christ.

"As I listened, it became clear to me that Satan was alive, real and right there in the room with me. I could feel evil all around, and I knew he wanted to destroy my soul. A rush of Bible stories and verses went through my mind. Memories of lessons learned in Bible camp and Christian school came over me like a flash flood. I remembered John 3:16 word for word. I knew that sin was destroying my life and that I couldn't sink much lower. I knew too that I was being given another chance to have new life in Christ at age twenty-three. There on my bedroom floor in front of the TV, I broke into tears and wept bitterly. I asked Jesus Christ to make His life my life."

God had Trish's attention at last. She was far away, lost in the night, without God and without hope in the world. Who would have ever designed a more unlikely scenario for repentance and new life in Christ than a "chance" viewing of the *Oprah Winfrey Show*? Amazing! Yet the voice of God spoke to her through a non-Christian television program.

God Is Calling to the Ends of the Earth

George heard the Speaking Voice in a nearly fatal automobile crash. The son of a Baptist pastor, he spurned his father's faith and the church family that loved him. He went out to seek real life in the real world. When he almost lost the only life he had, he knew that the sounds of crunching metal and breaking bones were the sounds of God calling to him. He too went home. Home to his father and mother's house and home to the Father's house.

The interesting part of George's story is that he's Polish. The God who is everywhere and who always seeks His own is just as busy in Poland as He is in Maryland. Language barriers do not garble the voice of God as He continuously calls wandering children home.

George told me his story on a train platform in Katowice, Poland. Those were the days when the Iron Curtain was still up and Soviet soldiers swaggered through Poland like they owned the country. Those were the days when it was dangerous to your well-being and your economic future to be an evangelical Christian in Poland. Yet George spoke of his faith openly and without fear. Then we prayed, bowing our heads in public while others watched curiously.

Today George has finished seminary and is working in a ministry of books and music evangelism in Poland and throughout central Europe. He is bright, talented and well-trained. I think he will become a pastor like his father and will eventually become one of Poland's leading evangelicals. Will you remember to pray for George, a wanderer who came home?

If there is a lesson to be learned or relearned from the stories of Trish, George and all the others who have courageously told me about their pain and sorrows, it is the truth of the omnipresent, ever-speaking God.

Take hope, all you caring, loving, praying parents of prodigal children. God, who is in all places at the same time, never stops calling His wandering sheep to the fold. In one way or another, He will get their attention.

For those who are still on the journey, there is also hope. God is there, calling, speaking. If you look and listen, you will hear your name.

Epilogue

Four reasons for leaving, a half-dozen stories, some informal conversations and a couple of chapters about issues related to why people leave the Christian faith. Is that it?

Yes, that's it so far as the interviews, research, analysis and methodologies are concerned. I think I've touched on most of what goes on in the heads and hearts of kids, young adults and older adults who choose to walk away from their faith. And I think I've looked at most of the evidence gathered in large part from people who have been through the experience as well as from research.

The good news is that there is hope. Most people who leave find their way back to the Savior. My prayer is that the grief and pain inflicted on all can be avoided by understanding why it happens and by doing what we can to prevent it from happening. I also hope that those who are spiritually whole and strong can help those who are wandering to find their way home.

But there is one more thing. I have left it for last because I know how easily people who are hurting can be turned off by what seems to be religious talky-talky. Putting this chapter earlier would have run the risk of deflecting the reader either from reading the chapter or from finishing the book. I am aware that even here it will seem at first to be saying "the same old stuff" that dropouts believe never worked for them in the first place.

Christian clichés, quick fixes, or anything resembling them are the ultimate turn-off to those who leave as well as to their confused, pain-filled parents. Someone has appropriately called these glib offerings "answerism"—nifty little spiritual solutions to great personal suffering and deep spiritual problems. Can there be *anyone* who likes it?

I say this because I hope it will help you understand that what I am about to say is as carefully considered as anything I have written in this book. It is *not* answerism.

The Ultimate Reason People Leave the Faith

Ultimately, the reason people leave the Christian faith is because of a failed or failing relationship with Jesus Christ. After all the reasons for leaving are examined, after all the methodologies are employed and all the parenting guidelines are absorbed, there is one more consideration: Jesus Christ and the cross. Calvary and the empty tomb.

If one day you hear that Tom Bisset gave up on Christianity, rejected his faith and wandered far from God, you will know, after all the talking and analyzing is finished, that somewhere, somehow, Tom Bisset turned his eyes from Jesus Christ and began depending on something else for his Christian life.

Maybe I started trusting my theology rather than my Lord. Put my faith in my faith. Believed in my beliefs. That will empty your soul before too long.

Or perhaps it was methodology. Spiritual mechanics. I could certainly indulge in that diversion given the numerous ways of preventing faith defection I have described in this book. For me, trusting in The Way could have slipped into trusting in the ways.

Then there's psychology. Instead of employing this useful science of the mind to help me understand my problems so I could then take them to Jesus and the atonement, I may have mistaken the bridesmaid for the Bride. Got obsessed with psyche and soul-gazing instead of gazing upon the cross where my Savior died for my sins and for my healing. Became client-centered instead of Christ-centered. All you have to do is read John White's *Putting the Soul Back Into Psychology*, or William Kilpatrick's *Psychological Seduction* to see how easily and subtly that can happen.

Perhaps my downward drift began when I put my confidence in my church and pastor, or Christian fellowship, or in seminars on how to live the Christian life or how to overcome spiritual afflictions and psychological addictions. Possibly I became a Christian conference cokie or a Christian media junkie with no real faith beliefs or authentic spiritual experiences of my own. Just looking, listening and saying amen.

Or I may have gotten sidetracked by life itself, taken my eyes off the Savior when a personal tragedy or triumph, or an agony or ecstacy came along to divert me from that *one basic reality* of the Christian life: Jesus Christ.

Trace back through the story of anyone who leaves the Christian faith and you will find, beneath all the real-life reasons people walk away, a failed relationship with Jesus Christ. Leaders or followers, beginners or seasoned saints, the process is the same. The soul's intimate and personal communion with Christ is shifted to something else, including good and useful things as well as the bad, and the leaving journey begins.

Certainly it is possible that some people who professed to be Christians never had an authentic relationship with Christ. Or they may have had a distorted, tortured relationship with the Lord based on a mistaken understanding of what it means to be a Christian. We've heard from enough leavers to know how destructive that kind of faith experience can be. But the point remains: A failing or failed relationship with Jesus Christ lies at the root—at the bottom of the bottom—of every troubled soul who decides to walk away from the Christian faith.

The End of the Line

Ultimately, faith rejection is about spiritual warfare. It is about Satan desiring to destroy us and our children. If you don't believe that, take time to talk in depth with people who have seriously rejected their faith.

In his excellent book *Spiritual Depression: Its Causes and Its Cures*, D. Martyn Lloyd-Jones examines the causes of spiritual depression and the "joyless Christianity" that characterizes much of modern Christian living. Even though he carefully offers thoughtful, biblically based "cures" to the various causes of spiritual depression, Dr. Lloyd-Jones is equally careful to conclude his study with a chapter he calls, "The Final Cure." It is as if, after wrestling with the varied aspects of depression and after offering the best biblical and practical wisdom possible, Dr. Lloyd-Jones turns at last to his best and brightest stratagem.

And just what is this final cure? It is, he says, "that I am made strong for all things in the One who constantly is infusing strength into me . . . That is the point to which [the apostle Paul] always brings every argument and discussion. Everything always ends in Christ and with Christ."[1]

For all the wanderers and leavers of all the ages, this is the end of the line. No matter what one's background or environment, no matter how justified one may be from a human standpoint in rejecting the Christian faith, there is only one question every dropout must face: What about Jesus Christ? All the well-intentioned analyses along with all the methods and strategies aimed at preventing faith rejection are background material.

So then, shall we all become mystics with our heads in the clouds, straining for a glimpse of Jesus? Shall we believe that if we are spiritual enough, if we can but trust God fully, all our problems are over? No, we must not give in to this lopsided view of the Christian life. It seldom works in real life. If it should turn out that children of such single-minded saints follow God with all their hearts, it will be possible to sift through their story and find that their parents employed, knowingly or unknowingly, many if not all of the attitudes, actions and methods talked about in this book.

Part of my reason for closing with these thoughts is that I hope it will help Christian parents understand that we must take care of our own spiritual health before we can pass a strong, vigorous faith on to our children.

One of the persistent themes of faith strugglers was their recognition of the reality of Christ in their parents' lives. No matter how confused or angry they were about the gospel as it was taught and practiced in their homes and churches, these dropouts could not get away from the soul-piercing reality of Jesus Christ in the lives of their parents. In some cases, the only thing they could remember about their homes, spiritually speaking, was their father and mother praying on their knees.

Once again, Dr. Lloyd-Jones goes to the heart of the issue. For him the answer is basics, basics, basics:

> There are no shortcuts in the Christian life. What I have to do is go to Christ. I must spend my time with Him, I must meditate upon Him, I must get to know Him. I must maintain my contact and communion with Christ and I must concentrate on knowing Him. I must do exactly what He tells me. I must read my Bible, I must exercise, I must practice the Christian life, I must live the Christian life in all its fullness.[2]

This alone, says Dr. Lloyd-Jones, is how Christ infuses His life and strength in us. This is how spiritual obstacles are ultimately overcome. Those who seek to help spiritual wanderers must realize that the final place of safety, the only source of healing and deliverance, is in Jesus Christ. It is a message as old as the gospel story. How very well we know it; how seldom we apply it.

And so I have come full circle. I am finished writing and I am back at Chapter 1. What I hope for, what I pray will happen, is that Christian parents will be able to find the balance between wisely doing their part in seeking to prevent their children from leaving the faith and faithfully trusting God to do His part.

Notes

Introduction

1. Edmund S. Morgan, *The Puritan Family* (New York: Harper & Row, 1944).

Chapter One

1. See *Falling From the Faith: Causes and Consequences of Religious Apostasy* by David G. Bromley (Newbury Park, CA: Sage Publications, 1988).

Chapter Three

1. See *Scaling the Secular City* by J. P. Moreland (Grand Rapids, MI: Baker Book House, 1987); and *Christianity and the Nature of Science* by J. P. Moreland (Grand Rapids, MI: Baker Book House, 1989).

Chapter Five

1. Charles Swindoll, *Dropping Your Guard* (Waco, TX: Word Books, 1983).

2. Associated Press newswire (March 18, 1991).

Chapter Seven

1. Perry Miller, *Jonathan Edwards* (Cleveland, OH: World Publishing Company, 1959).

2. The idea of the home as a safe haven first came to my attention in *Haven in a Heartless World* by Professor Christopher Lasch (New York, Basic Books, Inc., 1977). Lasch's book is not specifically Christian, but it makes numerous salient points regarding the importance of home and family. Lasch believes that the family mediates between social conditions and individual experience, shapes the individual's perception of the world and provides the mechanisms by which people deal with the world (p. 160).

3. Alan Bloom, *The Closing of the American Mind* (New York: Simon and Schuster, 1987), p. 56.

4. Frank E. Gaebelein, "The Educating Power of the Bible," *A Varied Harvest* (Grand Rapids, MI: William B. Eerdmans Publishing Co., 1967), p. 35.

5. Gaebelein, p. 37.

Chapter Nine

1. Telephone interview with Dr. David Allen, August 28, 1991.

2. Guy Greenfield, *The Wounded Parent* (Grand Rapids, MI: Baker Book House, 1990), p. 94. Greenfield's book is an excellent resource for hurting parents who are trying to understand their wayward children and who are seeking to rebuild broken relationships.

3. Robert Dudley, "Adolescent Heresy: The Rejection of Parental Religious Values," *Andrews University Seminary Studies*, Vol. 21, No. 1 (Berrien Springs, MI: Andrews University Press, Spring 1983).

4. Dudley, p. 59.

5. Dudley, p. 58.

6. Roy Zuck and Gene Getz, *Christian Youth: An In-Depth Study* (Chicago, IL: Moody Press, 1968)

Chapter Ten

1. C. K. Hadaway and Wade C. Roof, "Apostasy in American Churches: Evidence From National Survey Data," *Falling From the Faith: Causes and Consequences of Religious Apostasy* (Newbury Park, CA: Sage Publications, 1988), p. 38.

2. Hadaway and Roof, p. 45.

3. "The Wobegon Preacher"*Leadership* (Fall Quarter 1991), p. 53.

4. Author of article unnamed, p. 53.

5. Much excellent work has been done in this area by

qualified Christian researchers. There is also a great deal of material written by ex-gays who are living committed Christian lives. A catalog of the Christian books available on the subject can be obtained by writing Regeneration, Box 9830, Baltimore, MD 21284.

Chapter Eleven

1. Ross Campbell, *Kids Who Follow, Kids Who Don't* (Wheaton, IL: Victor Books, 1989).

2. Campbell, p. 41.

3. Campbell, p. 52.

4. Campbell, p. 53.

5. Campbell, p. 87.

6. Dr. Campbell includes a chapter on parents understanding themselves as part of this process. He calls it, "Parent, Know Thyself."

7. Commentary note, *The Jerusalem Bible* (Garden City, NY: Doubleday and Company 1966), p. 963.

Chapter Twelve

1. Oswald Chambers, *Oswald Chambers: The Best From All His Books*, Vol. 2 (Nashville, TN: Oliver-Nelson, 1989), p. 184.

Chapter Thirteen

1. James C. Dobson, *Parenting Isn't for Cowards* (Waco, TX: Word Books, 1987), pp. 49-50.

2. Stan Albrecht, Marie Cornwall and Perry Cunningham, "Religious Leave-Taking and Disaffiliation Among Mormons," *Falling From the Faith: Causes and Consequences of Religious Apostasy*, David G. Bromley, ed. (Newbury Park, CA: Sage Publications, 1988), p. 70. See also, Dean R. Hoge, "Why Catholics Drop Out," pp. 81-99; Eileen Barker, "Defection From the Unification Church," pp. 166-84; and Lynn D. Nelson and David G. Bromley, "Another Look at Conversion and Defection in Conservative Churches," pp. 47-61, *Falling From the Faith: Causes*

and Consequences of Religious Apostasy, David G. Bromley, ed. (Newbury Park, CA: Sage Publications, 1988).

3. Nelson and Bromley, p. 56.

Chapter Fourteen

1. John White, *Parents in Pain* (Downers Grove, IL: InterVarsity Press, 1979), p. 15.

2. Vance Havner, "Faith and Trouble," *In Tune With Heaven* (Grand Rapids, MI: Baker Book House, 1990), p. 194.

Chapter Seventeen

1. A. W. Tozer, *The Pursuit of God* (Wheaton, IL: Tyndale House Publishers, special edition), p. 74.

2. Tozer, p. 73.

Epilogue

1. D. Martyn Lloyd-Jones, *Spiritual Depression: Its Causes and Its Cure* (Grand Rapids, MI: Wm. B. Eerdmans Publishing Co., 1965), p. 291.

2. Lloyd-Jones, pp. 298-99, condensed.

To contact author write:

Tom Bisset
P.O. Box 9012
Lutherville, Maryland 21094